GETTYSBURG:
STORIES OF MEN AND MONUMENTS
AS TOLD BY BATTLEFIELD GUIDES

In 1913, the veterans returned to Gettysburg for the Fiftieth Anniversary of the battle. Dismayed by the inaccurate information that was dispersed, the aging soldiers lobbied for a program to insure the visitor to Gettysburg receive the proper information.

The first exam was given in 1915, to prospective Battlefield Guides. The National Park Service currently tests and licenses individuals to insure that accurate information is given to the visitor. The veterans who returned in 1913 were deeply concerned that the battlefield be preserved and the events that took place at Gettysburg were passed on to future generations. Today the tradition is carried on by the Licensed Battlefield Guides.

GETTYSBURG: STORIES OF MEN AND MONUMENTS

AS TOLD BY BATTLEFIELD GUIDES

Text By FREDERICK W. HAWTHORNE

Maps By DON MCLAUGHLIN

Photographs By ROY FRAMPTON
FRED HAWTHORNE
WALTER LANE
DON MCLAUGHLIN
DEB NOVOTNY
KATHY SHOWVAKER

Published by
THE ASSOCIATION OF LICENSED BATTLEFIELD GUIDES
PO Box 4152
Gettysburg PA 17325

Cover Illustration. Dawn on Cemetery Ridge, Gettysburg Battlefield

Copyright © 1988 by the Association of Licensed Battlefield Guides

Gettysburg: Stories of Men and Monuments
by Frederick W. Hawthorne

Published by the Association of Licensed Battlefield Guides

ISBN 0-9657444-0-x   *Printed in the United States of America*

CONTENTS

ACKNOWLEDGEMENTS

Projects such as this one seem quite easy to undertake at the time of inception. In reality it represents the combined efforts of a variety of individuals to bring it to fruition.

First, I would like to express gratitude to my fellow Licensed Guides, past and present, who have been lovingly interpreting this battlefield for many years. Few people know more about this park and what happened here. Many of the stories contained in these accounts have been told on tours of this field since the 1860's and Guides have freely exchanged, shared, and passed on many stories.

One of the main objectives of placing these in print was to attempt to document as many as possible. The resources of the Gettysburg National Military Park were invaluable in achieving this goal and Mr. Robert Prosperi was indispensable in providing guidance while using the park's resources. The permission of the GNMP, Lane Studio, and the Adams County Historical Society to use photographs in their possession is also gratefully acknowledged.

Several individuals should be singled out for their contributions. Fellow guides Kathy Showvaker, Deb Novotny, Roy Frampton, Don McLaughlin, and George Shealer were all in on the project since the beginning and all made suggestions and comments that were valued and appreciated. Their efforts are particularly evident in the fine quality of many of the photographs. Don McLaughlin also contributed his cartographic skills in producing the maps used in this guide. This work would never have been completed without their assistance.

A special thank you goes to Tanya Day who patiently read the entire manuscript several times. She pointed out a variety of problems and phraseology that was second nature to a Guide, but perhaps obscure to the general public. She never hesitated to suggest corrections and improvements and for that I am grateful. Those defects that still remain are solely the result of the author's own stubbornness or forgetfulness.

INTRODUCTION

They stand silently, over thirteen-hundred of them, dotting the Gettysburg battlefield as they have for nearly a century. These bronze and granite monuments mark the positions where Americans fought the greatest battle this continent has seen. Erected primarily by the regimental survivors and built by many of the finest companies and sculptors of late nineteenth century America, they honor the men who fought, bled, and died on this twenty-five square miles of Pennsylvania countryside. The monuments were to serve a two-fold purpose: to honor comrades who died in the struggle, and to tell of their accomplishments long after the last survivors had passed on.

Beginning in 1867, when the veterans of the 1st Minnesota Infantry placed a memorial urn in the National Cemetery, the monumentation of this and other Civil War battlefields became an increasingly important goal. Twelve years later, the regimental association of the 2nd Massachusetts Infantry placed a tablet at the edge of Spangler's Meadow to honor the men of the unit who died in action at that site. The following year the men of the 91st Pennsylvania placed a granite monument on Little Round Top to commemorate their services.

The approach of the twenty-fifth anniversary of the battle gave a push to the monumentation of Gettysburg. Veterans were now being assisted financially through the use of state appropriations earmarked specifically for monument construction. By the turn of the century, each northern state that had troops at Gettysburg had passed bills appropriating funds ranging from Indiana and Wisconsin's $3,000 to Pennsylvania's $400,000. Northern states at Gettysburg were well represented with monuments on the field.

In the years following the fiftieth anniversary in 1913, southern states became interested in honoring their citizens who fought and died in this climactic battle. Lack of available funding, the age of the South's surviving veterans, and a degree of opposition from their former enemies, made it impossible to consider building large numbers of individual regimental monuments. Instead, the goal of southern states became one of creating a single memorial designed to honor the sacrifice of all soldiers from each state. Virginia became the first to do so with the erection of its impressive memorial in 1917. The completion of the Tennessee State Memorial in 1982 finally gave each southern state a representative memorial at Gettysburg.

The process of monumentation is by no means complete as the approach of another anniversary has led to still more groups wishing to place monuments to fill "gaps" in the historic record. Currently, plans are being developed to place portrait statues on the field to honor two "forgotten" Union generals from Pennsylvania: Brig. Gen. John Gibbon and Brig. Gen. Samuel W. Crawford. Perhaps this will spur southern groups to work towards honoring some of the fine Confederate officers who performed well at Gettysburg. As of now, General Robert E. Lee remains the only southern officer to be portrayed as a statue on the field.

Today, the visitor to the park is met with the sight of hundreds of monuments, memorials, commemorative plaques, portrait and equestrian statues. The ravages of time, the elements, vandals, and negligence are beginning to take their toll. The government that pledged to these veterans to protect and care for each monument in perpetuity, consistently fails to provide the funds necessary to do so. In many ways, the very numbers that make upkeep and maintenance so difficult, also serves to defeat the original desire of the veterans. As more were erected the large quantity made it virtually impossible to see each one so all but the largest or most unusual, fade into the background. Few maps exist to show the location of specific memorials and those that do are not available to the general public. Adventuresome souls who wander the field seeking the monument of a particular unit or regiments from specific states, are soon discouraged by the scope of the task they have embarked upon.

Even when specific monuments are sought out and viewed by the visitor, no key exists to help understand what people see. The names of men portrayed and honored, once familiar to all, have simply become faces in bronze or names on a stone. The features, accoutrements, and designs, carefully created in bronze and granite and so meaningful to the old men who gathered around when they were dedicated, are now simply meaningless parts of the whole. Even the locations, so important that the legal system sometimes had to determine monument placements, have no significance to the average visitor. The fields, the roads, and the hills on which they were erected hold no special meaning. Over the years the significance of location, the importance of the names, and the symbolism of the features, have been lost to all except a handful of Licensed Guides, who incorporate much of this into their tours of the field, and the occasional Civil War buff, who relishes all aspects of this fascinating period.

Tour-books published in recent years concentrate exclusively on the events of the battle with the monuments receiving scant attention. Those studies dealing specifically with the monuments focus on attempting to publish a photograph of each one or compiling a complete listing of inscriptions. Value exists in both approaches.

This book has been developed with the average visitor in mind. It does not deal with the overall view of the battle, great leaders, or significant movements. It will not relate a history of the monumentation of this or other battlefields. Nor will you find a detailed listing of each inscription. This book is designed to give the reader a sampling of the monuments on the field and the story of the men who brought them into existence. It tells of the men who are portrayed, the equipment they used, the uniforms they wore, the animals they loved, the scenes they witnessed.

Due to space limitations not all monuments could be included and it became an arduous task to decide which would and would not. To be included, a monument had to be located along the park's chronological tour route. This immediately eliminated many fine memorials and interesting stories. Hopefully, these will be covered in a future study. As visitors to Gettysburg come from throughout the United States, an additional consideration was to include at least one monument from each state, North and South, that participated in the battle. The author hopes that the omission of any favorite story or particular unit will offend no one.

On October 3, 1889 the veterans of the 1st Maine Cavalry met at Gettysburg to dedicate their monument. The orator that day was the man who commanded the unit during the battle, Brevet Major General Charles H. Smith. In his speech he talked of the memorials at Gettysburg and their value for future visitors:

. . . these monuments, their emblems and legends that mournfully decorate this great battlefield from front to rear, from flank to flank, will become his interpreters and assistants.

The hope of the author is that this guide will provide the visitor with a key to understand and appreciate the physical legacy of those soldiers. Ultimately, that it will enable one to use the Gettysburg monuments as "interpreters" to understand how the men they honor lived, how they fought, how they died, and what their efforts contributed to future generations of Americans.

HOW TO USE THIS GUIDE

This book is designed to serve a dual purpose: one may simply read it for human interest stories relating to the Gettysburg monuments, or actually use it as a guide while touring the field. It is arranged following a chronological tour route through the battlefield. Monuments are discussed in the order they appear while traveling along the park's auto tour route. The field is divided into six sections, each of which can be visited separately and in any order. A map of the entire battlefield appears on page ten showing the main avenues and the location of the six sections. The first page of each section consists of a more detailed map of that part of the field. Each shows the relative location of the monuments included from that area.

Section One deals with selected memorials on the first day's battlefield west of town along the line of the Union First Army Corps. The omission of the Eleventh Corps line was not due to the lack of beautiful monuments or interesting stories, but rather the fact that this part of the field is not included in the park's chronological tour route. All southern state memorials, located along West and South Confederate Avenues, are covered in Section Two. The third section of the book covers the region where Lieutenant General James Longstreet's corps of the Army of Northern Virginia smashed the Union left on the afternoon of July 2, 1863. Section Four deals with the monuments commemorating regimental participation in the evening fight for Culp's and Cemetery hills. Memorials along the center of the Union line, where General Lee focused his last assault, are described in Section Five. The last section of the book is devoted to several important monuments located in the National Cemetery.

Due to the repetition involved, one feature has been left out of many of the accounts: the geometric designs that appear in most monuments. These are the individual regiment's corps badges. An earlier commander of the Army of the Potomac, Major General Joseph Hooker, ordered all soldiers to wear distinctive, color-coded badges to designate unit affiliation. In most cases these became such a part of the unit's heritage that the veterans proudly incorporated them into the monument's design. The symbols used to designate each corps were: First Corps—Disc or "Full Moon", Second Corps—Trefoil, Third Corps—Lozenge or Diamond, Fifth Corps—Maltese Cross, Sixth Corps—Greek Cross, Eleventh Corps—Crescent, Twelfth Corps—Star. To further delineate unit affiliation, colors indicated what division the unit was a part of: first division—red, second division—white, third division—blue, and fourth division—light green. In some cases this color scheme was incorporated in the unit monument. As you tour the field you may easily identify which corps a particular regiment was associated with simply by locating the badge incorporated in the monument. In addition to the corps badges the men usually wore a brass insignia denoting their branch of service and these occasionally appear on the monument. An upturned bugle represented the infantry, crossed cannon—artillery, and crossed sabres—cavalry.

Other common features used in the design of many monuments are carved oak leaves, laurel leaves, and palm fronds. The oak is symbolic of strength, the laurel of victory, and the palm of peace. Unfortunately such details are not easily seen in a photograph. If you are using this guide while touring the field, and you have the time, look at all sides of the monument. Many interesting features and inscriptions are on the sides that cannot be seen from the road.

PHOTOGRAPH CREDITS

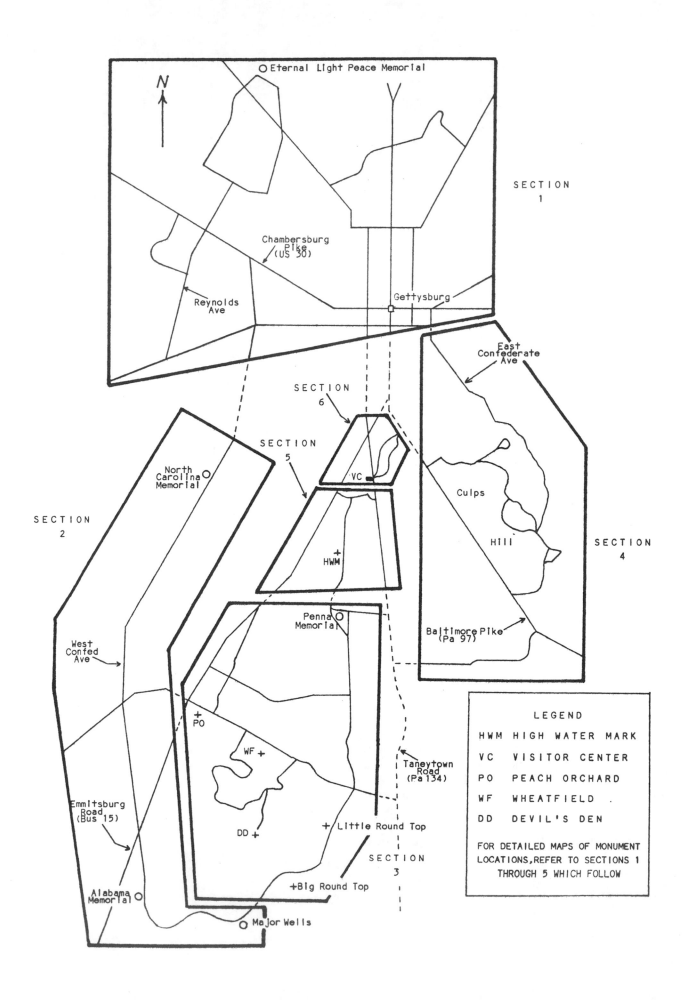

SECTION 1

SECTION 2

SECTION 3

SECTION 4

SECTION 5

SECTION 6

Eternal Light Peace Memorial

Chambersburg Pike (US 30)

Reynolds Ave

Gettysburg

East Confederate Ave

North Carolina Memorial

VC

Culps

Hill

West Confed Ave

Penna Memorial

Baltimore Pike (Pa 97)

+ HWM

+ PO

WF +

Taneytown Road (Pa 134)

Emmitsburg Road (Bus 15)

DD +

+ Little Round Top

+ Big Round Top

Alabama Memorial

Major Wells

LEGEND

HWM HIGH WATER MARK

VC VISITOR CENTER

PO PEACH ORCHARD

WF WHEATFIELD

DD DEVIL'S DEN

FOR DETAILED MAPS OF MONUMENT
LOCATIONS, REFER TO SECTIONS 1
THROUGH 5 WHICH FOLLOW

SECTION ONE: THE FIRST DAY'S BATTLEFIELD

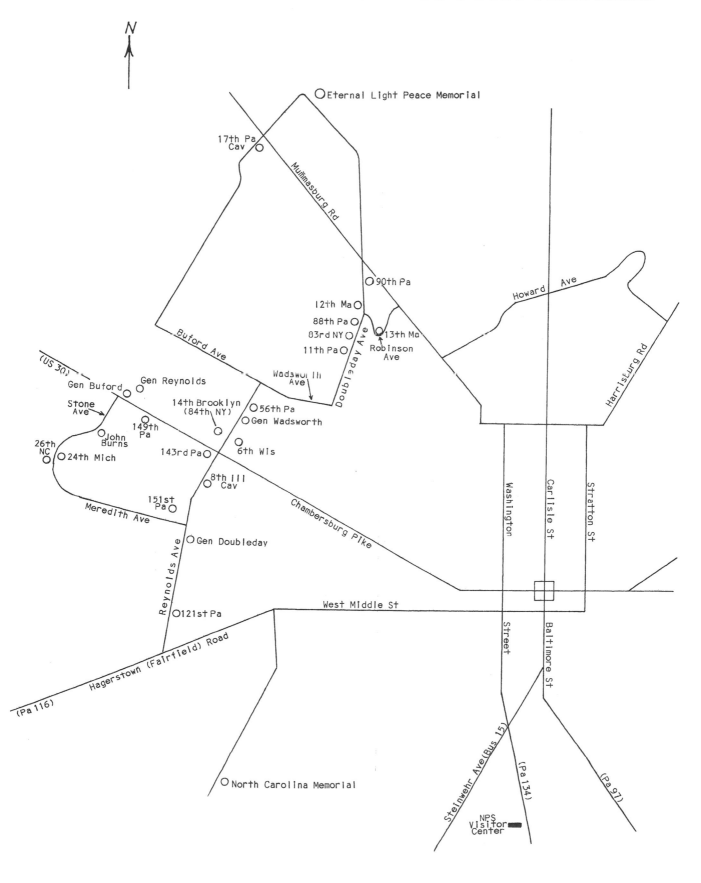

8th Illinois Cavalry

The 8th Illinois Cavalry monument is one of three erected by Illinois in 1891 to honor the state's regiments. It stands on the spot previously occupied by the 8th New York Cavalry monument which was moved in order to accurately mark cavalry positions. That of the 8th Illinois now marks the approximate center of the unit's main battle line on the morning of July 1, 1863.[1]

Carved from three blocks of Blue Westerly Rhode Island Granite, the design was developed by Smith Granite Company.[2] The most prominent feature is the regulation cavalry saddle carved out of the capstone. It is a complete replica down to the essential items of any cavalryman: his army blanket roll, haversack and saddlebags.

Although the monument was created to honor all members of the regiment, two individuals were given special recognition. The name of Lt. Marcellus Jones is carved on the front and the name of Private David Diffenbaugh is found on the back. Both were justifiably singled out by their comrades for inclusion on the monument. That July morning Lt. Jones of Company E was in charge of the picket detail at the Marsh Creek Bridge, about two miles to the west of the monument. At dawn he fired the first shot of the battle around 7:30 A.M. at approaching Confederates of General Heth's division.[3] This spot is today marked by a small five foot shaft of Napierville Illi-nois granite. It was placed there by Lt. Jones and two companions in 1886.[4] Difficult and somewhat dangerous to locate today, it marks the spot where one of the great battles of all time began.

Although no explanation is given on the monument for the presence of Private Diffenbaugh's name, it was placed there because he was the regiment's sole fatality at Gettysburg. This fact may appear odd due to the bloodiness of the battle, but cavalry was an expensive branch of the service to train and maintain; cavalrymen were therefore considered to be far too valuable to sacrifice in a pitched battle with enemy infantry. The role of Buford's Cavalry Division that morning was to fight a delaying action, holding key positions until infantry support arrived. Private Diffenbaugh gave his life performing that duty. Today he lies a short distance away from the monument that records his sacrifice, buried in Row A, Grave Four of the Illinois section of the National Cemetery.

[1] John L. Beveridge, David B. Vaughan, Joseph B. Greenhut, *Illinois at Gettysburg: The Final Report of the Battlefield Commissioners* (Springfield: H. W. Rokker, State Printer and Binder, 1892), p. 7.
[2] Ibid., pp. 7–8.
[3] Ibid., p. 18.
[4] Ibid., p. 18.

LS

LOCATION: REYNOLDS AVENUE
             (SOUTH OF ROUTE 30)
DEDICATED: SEPTEMBER 3, 1891
COST: $1500
DESIGN & CONTRACTOR: SMITH GRANITE
                      COMPANY
MATERIAL: BLUE WESTERLY GRANITE
           STANDARD BRONZE
SPECIFICATIONS: BASE–4'10"L × 3'2"W × 1'H
                 DIE–3'10"L × 2'2"W × 4'7"H
                 CAP–4'3"L × 3'8"W × 2'4"H

Abner Doubleday Portrait Statue

The portrait statue of General Abner Doubleday posthumously honors the vital role he performed for the Union cause on the first day of the battle. Known more for the much-disputed legend that he founded the game of baseball, Doubleday was a career army officer. As an artillery Captain in 1861 stationed at Fort Sumter in Charleston Harbor, he aimed and fired the first Union cannon shot of the Civil War in reply to the bombarding Confederate batteries.[1]

Unfortunately his finest hour of commanding troops in a battle would also be his last. After the death of his corps commander, John F. Reynolds, Doubleday took command of the First Corps and stubbornly defended the ground west of Gettysburg until his units were decimated and overwhelmed. A biased report from Eleventh Corps commander Oliver O. Howard stating that the First Corps had broken led to Doubleday's removal from his temporary command position. Feeling the sting of this censure, four days after the battle he asked to be relieved of command of his division. Much of his remaining life would be spent defending his role on that July day at Gettysburg.

Nearly a quarter century after his death in 1893 the state of New York commissioned sculptor J. Massey Rhind to create this memorial. It was unveiled by the General's niece, Alice Seymour Doubleday, on September 25, 1917 on a site which approximates the center of the line held by his division.[2] The statue overlooks the field on which Doubleday greatly contributed to slowing the advance of the Confederate army laying the groundwork for the eventual Union victory.

[1] Division of Publications, National Park Service *Fort Sumter: Anvil of War*, (Washington, D.C.: Government Printing Office, 1984), p. 26.
[2] Wayne Craven, *The Sculptures at Gettysburg*, (Eastern Acorn Press, 1982), p. 59.

LOCATION: AT INTERSECTION OF MEREDITH AVENUE AND SOUTH REYNOLDS AVENUE
DEDICATED: SEPTEMBER 25, 1917
COST: $7257
SCULPTOR: J. MASSEY RHIND
CONTRACTOR: (BRONZE) JONATHAN WILLIAMS FOUNDRY
(GRANITE) WORDEN-GILBOY CO. BATAVIA
MATERIAL: STANDARD BRONZE

DWM

151st Pennsylvania (Schoolteacher's Regiment)

Just inside the eastern edge of Reynold's woods stands the monument of the 151st Pennsylvania Infantry. Simple in design and construction, this monument has little to attract attention on a field with many ornate memorials. The only ornamentation present are the polished circles on the capstone, symbols of the First Army Corps, and a sculpture of three bronze muskets. Yet the story of the 151st at this site is one of great gallantry.

The regiment was one of two Pennsylvania nine-month regiments present at the battle. It had been organized in the late fall of 1862 and with 113 teachers in the ranks earned the nickname "Schoolteacher's Regiment". Company D was composed almost entirely of instructors and students from the Lost Creek Academy, McAllisterville, Juniata County. The principal at that school, George McFarland, commanded the regiment here July 1.[1] At Gettysburg, the 467 officers and men of the 151st had less than a month remaining before discharge.

As you stand at the monument, the flank markers to the left and right mark the battle line of the unit as they prepared to meet the Confederate assault. Twenty paces to the front the 26th North Carolina halted and the two regiments exchanged devasting musketry volleys. During the course of the action, Colonel McFarland received a wound that would cost him his right leg. Many of his regiment would remain here as casualties when the Union line fell back to the Seminary. One Confederate officer, passing over the position of the 151st, stated that "The dead of the enemy marked its line of battle with the accuracy of a line at dress parade".[2] Gettysburg cost the regiment 337 casualties, a majority occurring along this line.

Twenty-five years later to the exact hour, the survivors of the unit gathered to hear Colonel McFarland dedicate the monument to the memory of their fallen comrades. The three muskets on the front of the die are simple testimony of the brutal musketry fire the 151st both took and delivered that July afternoon.

[1] W. C. Storrick, *The Battle of Gettysburg: The Country, The Contestants, The Results*, 24th ed., (Harrisburg, Pa.: The McFarland Company, 1969), p. 22.

[2] See John M. Vanderslice, *Gettysburg Then and Now*, (New York: G. W. Dillingham, 1899; reprint ed., Dayton: Morningside Bookshop Press, 1983), p. 116.

REF

LOCATION: AT INTERSECTION OF MEREDITH
                AVENUE AND SOUTH REYNOLDS
                AVENUE
DEDICATED: JULY 1, 1888
COST: $1500
DESIGN & CONTRACTOR: P. F. EISENBROWN CO.
                BUREAU BROTHERS
MATERIAL: FULLER NEW HAMPSHIRE GRANITE
SPECIFICATIONS: 1ST BASE—5'8"SQ × 2'H
                2ND BASE—4'6"SQ × 1'8"H
                1ST DIE—4'SQ
                PLINTH—4'8"SQ × 1'4"H
                2ND DIE—3'SQ × 6'H
                CAP—3'8"SQ × 2'4"
                HEIGHT—17'4"H

26th North Carolina Infantry

Many fine Conderate regiments fought heroically during the battle of Gettysburg yet the exact positions where they fought largely remain unmarked. The south had suffered a crippling defeat here and commemorating that defeat was not a high priority. For decades after the war the poverty of the region made monument building financially difficult. Union veterans resisted the idea of their former enemies placing markers on the field. All of these combined to make Gettysburg a Union monumented battlefield park. Only one monument, the 2nd Maryland, was actually constructed through the efforts of a Confederate regiment's veteran's association. A second southern regimental marking, a plaque honoring the 4th Alabama, was placed through the efforts of one individual, a veteran of that unit.

A century would pass before the third southern regimental monument was erected, that of the 26th North Carolina Infantry. This unit participated in the assault on the Iron Brigade and other Union units in the area during the afternoon of July 1. In this action, they suffered heavy casualties. The 26th would ultimately lose 588 men, the greatest numeric loss sustained by any Confederate unit in this battle. Their monument, along with a companion marker on the scene of their battle position of July 3 at the angle, was erected through the sponsorship of the North Carolina Historical Commission and the state Department of Cultural Resources. Although this monument is not as artistic and ornate as many Union monuments, it nonetheless serves to honor the memory of equally brave Americans.

LOCATION: MEREDITH AVENUE
(REYNOLDS' WOODS)
DEDICATED: OCTOBER 5, 1985
DESIGNER/CONTRACTOR: KEYSTONE MEMORIALS
(BASE)
KARKADOULIAS
BRONZE
MATERIAL: SALISBURY PINK GRANITE
STANDARD BRONZE
SPECIFICATIONS: (BASE) 4'6"L × 4'W × 4'10"H
(PLAQUE) 30" × 36"

KLS

24th Michigan Infantry

Here, inside of Reynold's Woods, one of the more famous units of the Civil War fought. The 1st brigade of the 1st division, 1st Army Corps, was known popularly as the "Iron Brigade" for its steadfastness in battle. As you look at the monument to the newest regiment of that brigade, the 24th Michigan, you can see the statue of a typical infantryman. Rather than the kepi, the traditional fatigue hat worn by most regiments, the statue of the man is wearing a black, regulation army dress hat. This hat had a bell-crown, a wide brim turned up on the left side and secured with a brass eagle pin, and a black plume. It was proudly worn as a distinctive badge of honor by the men of the Iron Brigade.[1]

One legend that has persisted of the battle is that the Confederates attacking that morning truly belived that they were opposed by Pennsylvania militiamen. As most militia were hastily formed home-guard units, they rarely put up much more than token resistance when faced by battle hardened veterans. As these veteran Confederate soldiers advanced into the woods that morning they encountered the leading elements of the Iron Brigade. Noticing immediately the headgear of their adversary one was heard to remark "Taint no militia. There's them black-hatted fellers again. That's the Army of the Potomac!"[2]

For the black-hatted men of the 24th Michigan, on this July 1st and in these woods, their actions that day contributed heavily to the enhancement of the unit's image of a brigade made of iron. Stubbornly defending their position as long as possible, their stand that day would cost them dearly. By nightfall only ninety-nine men remained of the nearly five-hundred who had proudly marched to this line that morning. Their spirit and determination remains behind today embodied in the soldier in stone that tops the monument.

[1] See Vanderslice, *Gettysburg Then and Now*, p. 463; Donald L. Smith, *The 24th Michigan*, (Harrisburg: The Stackpole Company, 1962), p. 109.
[2] Smith, *24th Michigan*, p. 126.

FWH

LOCATION: MEREDITH AVENUE, REYNOLD'S
                WOODS
DEDICATED: JUNE 12, 1889
COST: $1350
DESIGNER/CONTRACTOR: RYEGATE GRANITE CO.
MATERIAL: WOODBURY GRANITE (BOTTOM)
              BARRE GRANITE (BASE–PLINTH)
              HARDWICK GRANITE (STATUE)
SPECIFICATIONS: 1ST BASE–5'5"SQ × 1'4"H
                2ND BASE–3'8"SQ × 15"H
                DIE–2'8"SQ × 3'H
                PLINTH–2'4"SQ × 25"H
                STATUE–7'H

John Burns Portrait Statue

John Burns was the only Gettysburg civilian known to have participated in the battle. Shortly after noon July 1, he approached Colonel Langhorne Wister of the 150th Pennsylvania Infantry and asked permission to fight with the unit. His appearance on the field supplied some comic relief to the soldiers witnessing the old man dressed in a dark, swallow-tailed coat, buff colored vest, dark trousers, and a high silk hat. The humor gave way to admiration as the men were inspired by the old man's spunk and courage. A veteran of the War of 1812, Burns fought alongside several Union regiments that afternoon receiving three wounds before being carried from the field.[1] Quickly recovering, the former borough constable spent the remaining eight years of his life living the part of the local hero.

Years after Burns' death the Pennsylvania General Assembly chose to honor his memory by erecting this statue at the site of his service.[2] The sculptor, Albert Bureau, designed and modeled a statue that captures the spirit and determination Burns exhibited as he strode across the McPherson Farm towards the firing line that afternoon. The details of the face were taken from a photograph.[3] On July 1, 1903 at 2:30 P.M., the statue was dedicated near the spot where Burns first joined the battle. Inscribed on the base are the words General Doubleday used in his official report to commend the heroism displayed by this citizen.

[1] Warren W. Hassler, Jr., *Crises at the Crossroads: The First Day at Gettysburg*, (University Park: University of Alabama Press, 1970), pp. 60–61.

[2] Board of Commissioners, *Pennsylvania at Gettysburg: Ceremonies at the Dedication of the Monuments*, 3 vols. (Harrisburg: William Stanley Ray, State Printer, 1914), 1:vii.

[3] Crave, *Sculptures at Gettysburg*, p. 69.

LOCATION: STONE AVENUE AT THE MCPHERSON FARM
DEDICATED: JULY 1, 1903
COST: $1500
SCULPTOR: ALBERT G. BUREAU
CONTRACTOR: BUREAU BROTHERS
MATERIAL: STANDARD BRONZE
SPECIFICATIONS: BASE IS A NATURAL GRANITE BOULDER FROM THE FIELD
TOTAL HEIGHT–6'1"

ACHS

LS

John Buford Portrait Statue

John Buford's statue stands vigilantly watching westward as he did that July morning in 1863 as the three thousand cavalrymen of his division prepared to meet the advance of Lee's army. A Kentuckian by birth, Buford fought the battle of his life using his small force effectively to blunt the advance of Heth's division. His task was to buy time for the oncoming Union infantry to arrive on the field. His efforts on McPherson's Ridge that morning contributed considerably to the final outcome of the battle. Unfortunately his career was cut short when he contracted typhoid fever in the fall of 1863 which brought about his death in December.[1]

Following the commemoration of the twenty-fifth anniversary of the battle in 1888, a group of the General's admirers met to form the Buford Memorial Assocation. Their purpose was to erect a suitable monument on the field to honor their former commander. During the discussion on design, John Calef, who had commanded a Horse Artillery battery under Buford's command, suggested that the design incorporate four Ordnance Rifles that were in the battery. Included was number 233, the same gun that had fired the first Union artillery shot of the battle under Buford's personal direction. Calef turned the serial numbers over to the Army Chief of Ordnance who tracked the tubes down and donated them to the committee.[2] They were then placed at the four corners of the base of the statue's pedestal. During the dedication ceremonies on July 1, 1895, Major Calef symbolically spiked the four tubes.[3]

[1] Ezra J. Warner, *Generals in Blue: The Lives of Union Commanders,* (Baton Rouge: Louisiana State University Press, 1964), pp. 52–53.

[2] John Calef, "Gettysburg Notes: The Opening Gun," *The Journal of the Military Service,* Vol. XL, March 15, 1876.

[3] To spike a gun meant to drive an iron spike into the vent and break it off. This rendered the gun inoperable and was usually done if the piece was in danger of being captured.

DWM

LOCATION: CHAMBERSBURG PIKE
DEDICATED: JULY 1, 1895
SCULPTOR: JAMES E. KELLY
CONTRACTOR: HENRY-BONNARD BRONZE
COMPANY
MATERIAL: STANDARD BRONZE

John Reynolds Equestrian Statue

Major General John Fulton Reynolds was among the first to fall during the battle of Gettysburg within four-hundred yards of the equestrian monument that honors him.[1] In command of the First Army Corps, his actions that morning in rushing the left wing of the Army of the Potomac to the field and selecting the ground for battle bought Army Commander Meade valuable time to consider his options. This statue was one of three equestrian statues authorized by the state of Pennsylvania to honor her sons in high army command. The "Reynolds" is unique in that it is a virtual engineering wonder. Weighing over nine thousand pounds, the horse and its rider are balanced on the pedestal with just two hoofs.[2] Traditionally it has been said that a code exists concerning the placement of the horse's hoofs on statues of this type. It is stated that two hoofs off of the ground indicate the death of the rider. One hoof off of the base indicates its rider received a wound during the battle, while a horse with all hoofs firmly planted on the ground would reflect the fact that the rider had survived. Although when applying this to the equestrian statues at Gettysburg one will find the tradition to hold true, it should be noted that some twenty years after creating the Reynolds Equestrian, the sculptor was specifically questioned about the tradition. He indicated that the positioning of the horse's hoofs beneath Reynolds was purely coincidental. Attempting to relay the rider's fate was not his intention in this monument.[3]

[1] This marker will be found just inside of Reynolds' woods near the monument of the 151st Pennsylvania Infantry.

[2] Craven, *Sculptures at Gettysburg*, p. 52.

[3] Letter, W. C. Storrick to Frederick Tilberg, National Park Historian, March 28, 1939. Concerns a conversation the writer had with the sculptor in 1915. Gettysburg National Military Park Files.

LOCATION: CHAMBERSBURG PIKE
DEDICATED: JULY 1, 1899
COST: $27,666
SCULPTOR: HENRY KIRKE BUSH-BROWN
CONTRACTOR: BUREAU BROTHERS
MATERIAL: STANDARD BRONZE

FWH

19

149th Pennsylvania Infantry

Along the Chambersburg Pike the monument honoring the 149th Pennsylvania Infantry identifies the spot defended by the unit July 1. The bronze bucktail on the side of the soldier's kepi marks the 149th as one of the "Bucktail Brigade." Other accoutrements complete the gear of the typical infantryman: the musket, bayonet, cartridge box, cap box, and canteen. The bronze pieces were actually placed on the monument shortly after its completion to replace parts the survivors felt were poorly carved from the original granite.[1] It exists today as evidence of the tremendous pride the men felt in their performance here and their desire to leave a permanent memorial for future generations.

It was here that one of the many episodes of personal heroism occurred. Early on the afternoon of July 1, as the 149th lay in a ditch alongside the Chambersburg Pike (where the monument stands today), the regiment began to receive heavy artillery fire from Oak Hill and Herr's Ridge. In order to draw off the fire, the color guard of the regiment,

under the direction of Color Sergeant Henry G. Brehm, took the flags and moved fifty yards to the north of the road. There they took cover behind a pile of fence rails while projectiles from over thirty cannon began to impact around them. They remained, drawing the artillery fire away from their comrades until the entire Union line on McPherson's Ridge began to give way. Sergeant Frank Price of the 42nd Mississippi Infantry took six comrades and stormed the isolated barricade. At that point the color guard decided to attempt to save the flags. Several of them were killed or wounded in the attempt to get away from the encircling enemy. Their heroism helped lessen the casualties the 149th would sustain that day. Today, the infantryman on the monument seemingly gazes towards the spot where the flags and their guard sat and waited.[2]

[1] Pennsylvania Monument Commission, "Pennsylvania at Gettysburg: Correspondence, Contracts, Designs, relating to the location and erection of the monuments and markers authorized by the General Assembly of the Commonwealth of Pennsylvania and erected under the authority of the Gettysburg Monument Commission," 1903, (after PaMC), Records pertaining to the monument of the 149th Pennsylvania Infantry.

[2] J. H. Bassler, "The Color Episode of the 149th Regiment of Pennsylvania Volunteers in the First Day's Fight at Gettysburg", Paper read before the Lebanon County Historical Society October 18, 1907, Reprint ed. (Butternut and Blue, 1983).

KLS

LOCATION: CHAMBERSBURG PIKE
              NEAR THE MCPHERSON BARN
DEDICATED: SEPTEMBER 11, 1889
COST: $1500
DESIGNED/CONTRACTOR: H. OURSLER & SONS
                              LATROBE, PA.
MATERIAL: BARRE GRANITE
             STANDARD BRONZE
SPECIFICATIONS: 1ST BASE–4'9"SQ × 2'0"H
                 2ND BASE–3'6"SQ × 1'3"H
                 FIGURE–2'6"SQ × 6'0"H

6th Wisconsin Infantry

The Montello Red Granite characteristic of the eight Wisconsin regimental monuments make them stand out on a field noted for many fine memorials. One of the Wisconsin regiments, the 6th, has its monument on the edge of a railroad cut, some distance from the other regiments of the "Iron Brigade". However, its association with the famed unit is noted by the Veteran's Badge of the brigade that forms the capstone and the unique hat of the organization etched on the front of the main die. The crossed muskets that also appear here served to remind many of the veterans who visited this spot of their old Belgian muskets. One veteran once commented that ". . . you could most always tell when they were fired by finding yourself on the ground"[1] The high polish of the granite serves to highlight the natural beauty of this native Wisconsin stone.

Beauty, however, would not have been a word to use when viewing this section of the field that July afternoon. The 6th Wisconsin was under the command of Lt. Colonel Rufus Dawes, a great grandson of William Dawes who, eighty-eight years before, had ridden with Paul Revere to warn the countryside around Boston.[2] Col Dawes' unit had been left in reserve as the rest of the Iron Brigade had been led into the battle earlier that morning. Around 11:00 A.M. the 6th Wisconsin had been sent over to the Chambersburg Pike to meet a potential threat from the vicinity of the railroad cut. At the pike they began to receive fire from several Mississippi regiments that had taken cover in the depression formed by the railroad bed. To meet this threat, Dawes, in conjunction with the 14th Brooklyn and the 95th New York, decided to charge. The 6th Wisconsin swept across the field in which their monument now stands and as they reached the cut they became involved in a vicious hand-to-hand fight. Corporal Lewis Eggleson of the regiment jumped down into the cut and seized the flag of the 2nd Mississippi. He was shot dead upon which a comrade used his musket to club Eggleson's assailant.[3] This was typical of dozens of small individual fights taking place all along the edge of the cut. Eventually a detachment of the 6th managed to get down across the eastern end of the cut in a

position to fire down the length of the depression. At this point Dawes called for the Confederates to surrender; some two hundred and fifty were then taken prisoner by the unit. The cost to the 6th was heavy. In the field behind and around the monument, the ground was littered with the dead, the dying, and the wounded of the unit. Out of the four hundred and twenty men who had jumped the fence at the pike moments before, two hundred and forty remained to reap the fruits of the victory at the cut.[4] Their monument today stands as a silent sentinel over this spot.

[1] Alan T. Nolan, *The Iron Brigade,* (Berrien Springs, Mich.: Hardscrabble Books, 1983), p. 18.

[2] Nolan, *Iron Brigade,* p. 14.

[3] Today Eggleson is buried in the Wisconsin section of the National Cemetery. Row C, grave number 15.

[4] Rufus R. Dawes, *Service with the Sixth Wisconsin Volunteers,* (Marietta, Ohio: E. R. Alderman and Sons, 1890), p. 168.

LOCATION: REYNOLDS AVENUE AT THE
        RAILROAD CUT
DEDICATED: JUNE 30, 1888
COST: $500
CONTRACTOR: B & M GRANITE CO
        MONTELLO, WISCONSIN
MATERIAL: MONTELLO GRANITE

DWM

14th Brooklyn (84th New York Infantry)

Across the road from the monument to the 6th Wisconsin stands the 84th New York Infantry monument. This regiment also had participated in the charge on the railroad cut that morning. Known popularly as the 14th Brooklyn, it was the only unit in the Union army to officially bear the name of a city.[1] Dressed in uniforms resembling the Chasseur a Pied, the old Light Infantry of the French army, the Brooklyn Chasseur's fierceness and determination in battle, earned respect from both sides during the war. Historically, the 14th was an old militia organization that traced its existence back to 1844. Such affection was shown by the citizens of the city towards their unit, that the memorial was erected using funds raised by donations from those citizens, and the seal of Brooklyn was prominently placed on the monument.

Atop the base is an eight foot high statue of a member of the 14th in the position of "handle car-

Harry W. Mitchell   *HISTORY OF THE FIGHTING 14TH*

tridge", one of the ten steps required in the loading of a muzzle-loading rifled musket.[2] Lieutenant Harry W. Mitchell, who was wounded during the battle, served as the model for the statue which was carved wearing the distinctive uniform of a Brooklyn Chasseur.[3] The kepi was red with the unit's numeral '14' on the front. The Chasseur coat was blue, trimmed in red, with three rows of brass buttons. The outer rows, on the blue material, were designed to give the appearance of this one garment being two, an open blue coat worn over a buttoned red shirt. Red trefoil epaulettes were worn on the shoulders by all ranks. Their trousers were also made of a red material and the uniform was completed by white, canvas gaiters which buttoned up on the side.[4] During the first major land battle of the Civil War, at Bull Run, the regiment's steadfast defense, and colorful uniform, led to their Confederate foes dubbing

LOCATION: NORTH REYNOLD'S AVENUE
               NEAR THE RAILROAD CUT
DEDICATED: OCTOBER 19, 1887
COST: $3510
SCULPTOR: R. D. BARR
MATERIAL: WESTERLY GRANITE
DESIGNER/CONTRACTOR: SMITH GRANITE CO.
STANDARD BRONZE
SPECIFICATIONS: BASE–9'0"SQ × 18'8"H
                        STATUE–2'3"SQ × 8'6"H
                        SEAL–1'6"DIA
                        TABLETS–1'6"DIA

DWM

them the "Red Legged Devils."[5] On many other fields throughout the war, particularly here at Gettysburg, the 14th Brooklyn would enhance the reputation earned at Bull Run.

[1] C. V. Tevis, *The History of the Fighting Fourteenth*, (New York: Brooklyn Eagle Press, 1911), p. 100.

[2] Berkeley R, Lewis, *Small Arms and Ammunition in the United States Service 1776–1865*, 3rd ed. (Washington, D.C.: Smithsonian Institution Press, 1968), p. 85. The ten steps were: LOAD, HANDLE CARTRIDGE, TEAR CARTRIDGE, CHARGE CARTRIDGE, DRAW RAMMER, RAM CARTRIDGE, RETURN RAMMER, CAST ABOUT, PRIME, SHOULDER ARMS. The minimum time required to load and fire would be 15 to 20 seconds.

[3] Kathleen R. Georg, *The Location of the Monuments, Markers, and Tablets on the Battlefield of Gettysburg*, (Gettysburg: Eastern National Parks and Monuments Association, 1982), p. 48.

[4] Philip J. Haythornthwaite, *Uniforms of the Civil War*, (New York: Macmillan Publishing Co., Inc., 1976), pp. 154–155.

[5] Anthony-Battillo, "Red Legged Devils from Brooklyn," *Civil War Times Illustrated*, February 1972, pp. 10–16.

James Wadsworth Portrait Statue

The portrait statue of James Samuel Wadsworth honors a man who commanded the first Union infantry division to go into action at Gettysburg. General Wadsworth was a wealthy fifty-three year old citizen of New York at the outbreak of the war. Extremely patriotic, he personally made arrangements to send two shiploads of supplies through to Maryland to aid in defending Washington during those uncertain early days of the war. Over $17,000 of his own money was contributed to this project.[1] Wadsworth eventually went to Washington to lend what aid he could to the Union cause. He was present at the Union defeat in the first major land battle of the war, Bull Run, in July, 1861. In the reorganization of the army that came in the aftermath of this defeat, Wadsworth was appointed Military Governor of Washington, D.C., a post he would hold for over a year.[2]

It was during his tenure as Military Governor that the background for an amazing series of events took place. In that first year of war, the capital was a hotbed of pro-southern sentiment and the Union authorities were kept constantly vigilant to potential

LOCATION: NORTH REYNOLDS AVENUE
DEDICATED: OCTOBER 6, 1914
COST: $7788.28
SCULPTOR: R. HINTON PERRY
DESIGNER: EDWARD P. CASEY (BASE)
CONTRACTOR: GORHAM MANUFACTURING CO
     (STATUE)
     NATIONAL GRANITE CO. (BASE)
MATERIAL: STANDARD BRONZE
    DARK BARRE GRANITE
SPECIFICATIONS: BASE–12'SQ
     DRUM–4'DIA × 3'H
     STATUE–9'H

DWM

threats. One Virginia farmer caught in this web of uncertain times was Patrick McCracken. Picked up by a military guard on suspicion of spying, McCracken was thrown into the Old Capital Prison without being formally charged. Some time passed before the case reached the attention of Wadsworth. He believed McCracken's version of the story and ordered him released. Finding that the man had spent his money and was without the means to return to Virginia, the General furnished him ample funds from his own pocket to continue his journey.[3]

In the fall of 1862, Wadsworth assumed field command of the 1st Division, 1st Corps, Army of the Potomac, the command he led into battle here July 1. The statue depicts General Wadsworth as he "... stood at Gettysburg, with one arm directing the placing of his troops so as to withstand a charge of the Confederates." Through the fall of 1863 and the winter of 1864, Wadsworth led his men capably. As the spring campaigning season approached, the paths of James Wadsworth and Patrick McCracken were set to cross one last time.

The Army of the Potomac plunged into the area known as the Wilderness in May of 1864, colliding head on with their old adversary, the Army of Northern Virginia. Into this tangled region Wadsworth again led his division. Hit by a Confederate flanking attack, his division crumbled. Wadsworth himself was severely wounded in the head and left lying on the field behind the Confederate lines. Carried to a field hospital in the rear, the wound was examined and pronounced fatal. Shortly after dark on May 7, Patrick McCracken, visiting the hospital to bring food and milk to the wounded from his nearby farm, came across the man who had helped him nearly two years before. The next morning when he again appeared in camp he secretly dropped a small package of food at Wadsworth's tent. There the General's companion, a Massachusetts doctor, Z. Boylston Adams, attempted to give him some milk. It was the last that Wadsworth would ever receive. When McCracken returned later that afternoon, he found that the General had died. He went to the Confederate surgeon in charge and asked permission to move the body to his own family burial ground. He then wrote to Mrs. Wadsworth to inform her of her husband's death and resting place. Later that month the General's body was removed and sent home to his family in New York. The old debt had been repaid.[4]

Today General Wadsworth's statue stands over the field at Gettysburg. It is not simply the representation of bronze of yet another soldier, but a noble man who in the midst of war found compassion for a fellow human being.

[1] New York Monuments Commission for the Battlefields of Gettysburg, Chattanooga, and Antietam, *In Memoriam, James Samuel Wadsworth, 1807–1864,* (Albany: J. B. Lyon Company, Printers, 1916), p. 83.

[2] Ibid., p. 86.

[3] Ibid., p. 52.

[4] Ibid., p. 116–120

56th Pennsylvania Infantry

The all-bronze monument of the 56th Pennsylvania Infantry honors the regiment credited with firing the first organized Union musketry volley of the battle. Part of the General Lysander Cutler's brigade was coming into line of battle to meet the advance of General Davis' Mississippi brigade. At approximately 10:15 A.M. one of Cutler's units, the 56th, managed to swing into a line of battle just seconds before the others and began firing at the enemy.

Their monument today is topped by an eight foot high stack of three Springfield rifled muskets with fixed bayonets, identical replicas of the weapons with which that first volley was fired. In the center of the muskets a furled and sheathed battle flag completes the design. The sculpture itself was meant to symbolize the completion of the soldiers' work, a fitting tribute to the veterans of the 56th and other units, whose efforts here contributed to the completion of the work.[1]

[1] *Pennsylvania at Gettysburg,* 1:347.

REF

LOCATION: NORTH REYNOLDS AVENUE
DEDICATED: SEPTEMBER 11, 1889
COST: $1500
DESIGN/CONTRACTOR: BUREAU BROTHERS
MATERIAL: STANDARD BRONZE
        VERMONT GRANITE (BASE)
SPECIFICATIONS: 40"DIA
        5/16" THICK
        16'2" TOT HT

17th Pennsylvania Cavalry

When the veterans of the 17th Pennsylvania Cavalry met in 1886 to discuss the possiblity of placing a monument at Gettysburg, they had three goals they wished to achieve. They wanted to construct a unique and different monument, one that would be typical of cavalry, and one that would last a long time. In looking at the result of their work, most would agree that they succeeded in achieving their goals.

At 2:00 P.M. on June 30, 1863 the 17th Pennsylvania entered Gettysburg, the first unit of the Army of the Potomac to do so.[1] Proceeding north of town, they sent out individual vedettes to cover the roads leading from the west and north. Vedettes served as the actual eyes of the army—seeking the enemy, sending intelligence back to army headquarters, and providing an early warning system. It was this typical cavalry role that these veterans chose to depict on their monument. The location also supported this, as the vedette of the 17th in this area was situated near the site of the present monument.[2]

Carved in bas relief on a twenty-seven ton block of Westerly granite is a lifesize mounted vedette portrayed as he looked "just discovering the enemy". His carbine is raised, ready to fire a shot to warn the cavalry reserve. The sculptor, an unknown artisan employed by Smith Granite Company, used as his model George W. Ferree, a veteran of Company L of the regiment. To assure accuracy, Ferree donned his original uniform and equipment which were faithfully reproduced on the face of the monument.[3] This attention to detail in accoutrements extends to such features as the end of a curry comb protruding from one of the saddlebags. In the design and the massiveness of the stone with which the sculptor worked, the unit did achieve a unique and different monument, a lasting memorial to the men of the 17th Pennsylvania.

[1] H. P. Moyer, *History of the Seventeenth Regiment Pennsylvania Volunteer Cavalry,* (Lebanon, Pa.: Sowers Printing Company, 1911), p. 49.

[2] Ibid., p. 373.

[3] Ibid., p. 374, 377.

LOCATION: BUFORD AVENUE /
                 MUMMASBURG ROAD
DEDICATED: SEPTEMBER 11, 1889
COST: $3500
DESIGN/CONTRACTOR: SMITH GRANITE CO.
MATERIAL: BLUE WESTERLY GRANITE
SPECIFICATIONS: 10'6"H
                       10'3"W
                       3"T
                       27 TONS

George W. Ferree

HISTORY OF THE 17TH PA

REF

Peace Light Memorial

In 1913, over fifty-five thousand northern and southern veterans came to Gettysburg to participate in a massive reunion celebrating the 50th anniversary of the battle. One outcome of this reunion was a desire among the veterans to construct a lasting symbol to the unity of the nation—a monument to peace.

Another twenty-five years would pass before their desire became a reality. The United States participated in a world war and survived a depression before the approach of the 75th anniversary spurred on efforts to complete the memorial. Contributions were solicited and eventually received from seven states: Pennsylvania, Virginia, Wisconsin, Illinois, Tennessee, New York, and Indiana. On July 3, 1938, as the climax of the last major reunion of Civil War veterans, the dedication ceremonies took place. People came from all parts of the country to witness the event. Estimates of those in attendance that day ranged from two hundred and fifty thousand to four hundred thousand. Included as honored guests were over eighteen hundred Civil War veterans, ranging in age from eighty-eight to one hundred and twelve years old.[1] All watched as Franklin Roosevelt dedicated the monument. Finally a gas-fed eternal flame was ignited in the urn atop the shaft by a Union veteran and a Confederate veteran.

Designed by Paul Phillipe Cret, the simple forty-foot high shaft is visible from many parts of the field. The base relief of the two women on the shaft was the work of Lee Lawrie. They are intended to represent the peace and good will existing between north and south. In front, the traditional symbol of the country, the eagle, completes the group.

One change that has been made over the years was the sacrifice of the symbolic flame of peace that was extinguished during the energy crises of the early 1970's. Relit briefly during the bicentennial it was permanently replaced by the present sodium vapor light in 1978.

[1] L. W. Minnigh, *Gettysburg: What They Did Here,* (Gettysburg: The Bookmart, 1954), p. 192.

LS

LOCATION: OAK HILL
DEDICATED: JULY 3, 1938
COST: $50,000
ARCHITECT: PAUL PHILIPPE CRET
SCULPTOR: LEE LAWRIE
CONTRACTOR: GEORGE A. FULLER CO.
MATERIAL: ALABAMA LIMESTONE
       CRAB ORCHARD FLAGSTONE
SPECIFICATIONS: PLATFORM—85'L × 42'W
       SHAFT—40'H
       BAS RELIEF—8'H

90th Pennsylvania Infantry

One of the most unusual monuments on the field at Gettysburg is the "stalwart oak tree" of the 90th Pennsylvania Infantry. Carved to represent a tree on the field that had been torn and shattered by artillery fire, bronze accoutrements, a knapsack, a rifled-musket, and a canteen are slung over one of the shattered branches. Ivy, also sculpted in bronze, has begun to climb the remaining trunk at the top of which is a bronze nest with baby birds resting inside. Perched on the nest, the mother watches over her brood. The intention was to symbolize a regeneration of life amidst the debris of battle and the start of a new era of peace and goodwill.[1]

A variation of the story behind this monument has been handed down through the years. No written source for it has yet been found. The story relates that during the heat of the battle one of the large oak trees near the position of the 90th Pennsylvania was hit by a shell and splintered. A large piece of the tree and many small branches came raining down on the men. On the ground among the debris, was a robin's nest filled with unharmed, but quite shaken babies. A soldier witnessing the scene picked up the nest. Under heavy fire and at great risk to his own life, the soldier climbed up the shattered stump and replaced the nest. Whether or not the incident actually took place, the tree and the nest combine to form a unique record of the 90th Pennsylvania's participation at Gettysburg.

[1] *Pennsylvania at Gettysburg*, 1:500.

LOCATION: DOUBLEDAY AVENUE
          AT THE MUMMASBURG ROAD
DEDICATED: SEPTEMBER 3, 1888
COST: $1500
DESIGNER/CONTRACTOR: JOHN M. GESSLER
          GRANITE AND
          MARBLE COMPANY
MATERIAL: LIGHT WESTERLY GRANITE
          STANDARD BRONZE
SPECIFICATIONS: DIAMETER–3'
          HEIGHT–14'

GNMP

12th and 13th Massachusetts Infantry

Massachusetts was the first state to appropriate funds to help their veteran's associations place monuments on the field at Gettysburg. Two fine ones, representing the 12th and 13th Massachusetts infantries, are located in the Oak Ridge area. Among the earliest markers erected, they often lack the complete inscriptions and battle narrative of the monuments that followed, yet they are among the most artistic on the field.

The monument to the 12th Massachusetts represents a large granite minie bullet partially wrapped in an American flag. Since the 12th was nicknamed the "Webster Regiment", a medallion likeness of Daniel Webster appears on the front. Webster's son Fletcher had commanded the unit until his death in the summer of 1862. Daniel Webster had been a staunch supporter of the Union in the early days of sectional crisis in this country. During one confrontation in the 1830's, he had challenged secession advocate John Calhoun with the phrase that surrounds the medallion . . . "Liberty and Union, Now and Forever, One and Inseparable!" The unit that bore Webster's name contributed greatly towards preserving the union he had verbally defended during his service in the Senate. At the base, the empty cartridge box and bayonet scabbard symbolize the completion of that work.[1]

Down the slope of the hill from the Webster Regiment stands the monument to the 13th Massachusetts Infantry. Although its lineage was not as deeply rooted in the history of the sectional tensions of the period, it was still a solid unit. Holding on to a very crucial position throughout that long afternoon, they fought well, pulling out only when further defense of the position was hopeless. Their monument is topped by a statue which represents the color sergeant of the unit. One story states that the color bearer depicted was killed on the spot now occupied by the monument.[2]

[1] Vanderslice, *Gettysburg Then and Now*, p. 411.
[2] Ibid., pp. 125, 411.

LS

LOCATION: DOUBLEDAY
DEDICATED: OCTOBER 8, 1885
COST: $500

LOCATION: ROBINSON AVENUE
DEDICATED: SEPTEMBER 25, 1885
COST: $500

88th Pennsylvania Infantry

On the afternoon of July 1, the 88th Pennsylvania Infantry aided in repelling the attack of Alfred Iverson's North Carolina brigade from this spot. In a subsequent counterattack, the regiment charged into the field beyond the woodline to the point now marked by a small stone. They succeeded in capturing a number of Iverson's men and the battleflags of the 23rd North Carolina and the 26th Alabama.[1]

The veteran's association of the 88th Pennsylvania was quite active in attempting to preserve the history of the unit on the field. In 1881, they placed three markers on the field to designate the positions held by the unit during the battle. These included the one out in the field near the main monument, one in Zeigler's grove near the Cyclorama Center, and a third on Cemetery Ridge south of the clump of trees.[2] When the state of Pennsylvania offered $1500 for each unit to place a monument on the field, the 88th chose to erect the one here on Oak Ridge.

Its design was suggested by the surviving members of the unit as a "remembrance of the suffering and sacrifice of the citizen-soldier".[3] The most prominent feature of the monument is the stack of war materials over which has been tossed the symbolic laurel wreath of victory. Atop the stack sits a large eagle with outstretched wings gazing over the field of battle. Containing nearly twenty different pieces of equipment a soldier would be familiar with, the monument is interesting to look at for a few minutes to see how many of these you can identify.

[1] *Pennsylvania at Gettysburg*, 1:482.

[2] John D. Vautier, *History of the 88th Pennsylvania Volunteers in the War for the Union, 1861–1865*, (Philadelphia: J.B. Lippencott Company, 1894), p. 217.

[3] *Pennsylvania at Gettysburg*, 1:487.

LOCATION: DOUBLEDAY AVENUE
DEDICATED: SEPTEMBER 11, 1889
COST: $3000
DESIGNED: MEMBERS OF THE REGIMENT
SCULPTOR: JOHN LACMER
COMPANY: MILLER AND LUCE (PEDESTAL)
MATERIAL: BASE–QUINCY GRANITE
          STATUE–CONCORD GRANITE
SPECIFICATIONS: 1ST BASE–8'4"L × 5'W × 2'3"H
          2ND BASE–7'L × 3'8"W × 1'10"H
          3RD BASE–6'4"L × 3'10"W × 1'H
          DIE–5'10"L × 2'6"W × 2'4"H
          CAP–6'4"L × 3'W × 1'2"H
          TROPHIES–6'L × 3'W × 7'H

REF

83rd New York Infantry

One of the most impressive monuments on the field at Gettysburg is the large shaft constructed to honor the men of the 83rd New York Infantry. The 83rd's history stretched back to the spring of 1850 when it was organized as the 9th New York State National Guard, a designation that appears on the memorial. Its services, of considerable importance in many battles of the Civil War, would extend well past the war.[1]

In the latter part of 1886, veterans from the unit had visited the field and noted the poor representation of New York monuments on the field. Only two had been erected by state units (14th Brooklyn and 124th New York) and neither of those represented veterans from New York City. Since a site for a monument had already been selected and a committee formed to oversee its construction, funds for the monument were solicited from friends and survivors of the regiment. By September of 1887, nearly $3500 had been collected. The following May the cornerstone was laid and within three weeks the monument was ready for dedication. This event would be one of the largest single monument dedications the area would witness as it was attended not only by the old veterans, but by many veterans of other First Corps units, several ranking officers from the battle, and the entire 9th New York National Guard sent by the Governor to honor their predecessors.[2]

The fifty-one foot tall shaft consists of alternating levels of red and white granite topped by a large bronze cannonball. Resting on the ball is a huge bronze eagle weighing seven hundred pounds with a wing span of nearly six feet. It was modeled after a specimen shot just a short time before the monument's creation. At the base of the shaft on a bronze medallion is the regimental badge and motto "Ratione Aut Vi," "By Reason or Force."

FWH

[1] William Todd, ed., *History of the Ninth Regiment, N.Y.S.M., N.G.S.N.Y (83rd New York Volunteers), 1845–1888*, (New York: George S. Hussey, 1889), pp. 4, 6, 9, 646–647.

[2] Ibid., pp. 641–647, 667, 669.

LOCATION: DOUBLEDAY AVENUE
DEDICATED: JULY 1, 1888
COST: $6000
SCULPTOR: J. G. HAMILTON
DESIGNER/CONTRACTOR: SMITH GRANITE CO.
MATERIAL: WESTERLY GRANITE
                 STANDARD BRONZE
SPECIFICATIONS: BASE–15'0"SQ
                 TOTAL HEIGHT–51'0"
                 EAGLE–5'8" WINGSPREAD
                 TABLETS–2'11" × 2'4"

11th Pennsylvania Infantry

Dedicated to the "heroic dead" of the unit, the monument constructed by the 11th Pennsylvania Infantry stands silently atop Oak Ridge at the spot they defended that afternoon of July 1. Driving along the row of monuments honoring the men of John Robinson's division, you will immediately see a fine bronze statue of a skirmisher preparing to fire sitting atop the 11th Pennsylvania monument. Few bother to get out and walk to the front where another bronze statue can be found, the statue of a small dog curled up as if sleeping. The dog—Sallie—was the mascot of the 11th and she too was numbered among the "heroic dead" to whom the monument was dedicated.[1]

Sallie had been given to the regiment as a puppy during the early days of the war. Growing up with the men of the unit, she became a comrade-in-arms, sharing the marches, the hardships, the extremes of the climate and the dangers of the battle. During battles, Sallie was known to take her position at the end of the line of battle, barking as loud as she could at the enemy. Of a friendly nature, Sallie was said to hate only three things: "Rebels, Democrats, and Women."

At Gettysburg, the little dog was with the men of the 11th Pennsylvania throughout the battle of July 1st. During the course of the retreat through the town, she became separated from the unit. Not knowing where they had gone, she remembered where they had been and worked her way back across the debris of the field to this ridge and her fallen comrades. There, amidst the wounded, the dying, and the dead, Sallie laid down and maintained a silent vigil over her friends for the remainder of the battle. After the Confederate retreat a member of the 12th Massachusetts found her still lying among the dead, weak from the lack of food, but alive. She was returned to her unit.

Recovering quickly, Sallie resumed her place in the regiment serving faithfully through the balance of the war. On February 6, 1865 within two months of the war's end she was going into battle with her unit at Hatcher's Run, Virginia. During the course of the fight she was shot through the head and killed. Such was the feeling of the men of the regiment towards their mascot that they buried her on the field despite the heavy enemy fire. Years later when designs for the regimental monument at Gettysburg was discussed it was felt only appropriate that their little pet, their friend, and their comrade be memorialized with the unit.[1]

[1] John D. Lippy, Jr. *The War Dog: A True Story*, (Harrisburg: The Telegraph Press, 1962).

LS

LOCATION: DOUBLEDAY AVENUE
COST: $2255
SCULPTOR: E. A. KRETSCHMAN
DESIGNER/CONTRACTOR: BUREAU BROTHERS
MATERIAL: STANDARD BRONZE
SPECIFICATIONS: BASE–4'9" × 4'7" × 1'2"
      PLINTH–3'9" × 3'7" × 10"
      DIE–3'5" × 3'3" × 5'
      STATUE BASE–2'3" × 2'1" × 3"
      STATUE HEIGHT–6'
      STATUE WEIGHT–1000 POUNDS

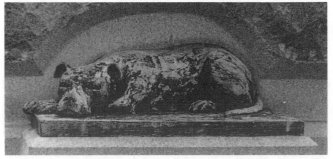

FWH

143rd Pennsylvania Infantry

Carved on the front of a single block of granite is a life-size bas relief of a soldier in the unusual pose of shaking his fist at something. The soldier depicted was Color Sergeant Ben Crippen of the 143rd Pennsylvania Infantry and his gallantry was noted by friend and foe alike.

Crippen had been in the army less than a year as his regiment headed north into his home state that summer. While the battle swirled around the McPherson farm, his job as the bearer of the national flag was to keep this vital symbol of the unit, the heart and soul of the regiment, where all eyes could see and rally around it. His 6'1" frame made the flag of the 143rd an even more prominent rallying point. Increasing pressure began to force the Union line back towards the Lutheran Seminary. Among the last of the unit to fall back was Sergeant Crippen who made a point of turning around periodically to defiantly shake his fist at the advancing Confederates.

His actions were witnessed by Confederate corps commander, Lieutenant General A. P. Hill who expressed his sorrow when he saw Crippen finally fall.[1]

The body of their heroic color bearer was never recovered and today he probably rests among the unknown in the National Cemetery. The survivors of the 143rd felt that his memory above all others should be singled out for recognition on the monument that honored them all. Nearly two-thirds of the $1500 total cost of the monument was devoted to the sculpting of a likeness of Ben Crippen standing forever in the pose that inspired and encouraged them on that unforgettable day.

[1] See Hassler, *Crises at the Crossroads*, pp. 116; J. Warren Gilbert, *The Blue and Gray: A History of the Conflicts During Lee's Invasion and Battle of Gettysburg*, (Gettysburg: The Bookmart, 1952), p. 50; *Pennsylvania at Gettysburg*, 2:702.

KLS

LOCATION: CHAMBERSBURG PIKE AND
             REYNOLDS AVENUE
DEDICATED: SEPTEMBER 11, 1889
COST: $1500
DESIGNER/CONTRACTOR: SMITH GRANITE CO.
MATERIAL: BLUE WESTERLY GRANITE
SPECIFICATIONS: BASE–5'0"L × 3'0"W
                    HEIGHT–8'0"

121st Pennsylvania Infantry

The design of the monument to the 121st Pennsylvania Infantry, like that of many others on the field, is tied to the accoutrements that were an everyday part of the soldiers life. The die of the monument is designed to form a large knapsack/blanket roll combination and by looking closely finely carved straps can be seen in the stone. Miscellaneous items in bronze, the kepi, sword, musket, cartridge box, and bayonet, also form part of the monument. Perhaps the most interesting features are the bursting shell shown in the upper left corner of the die and the American flag draped over the stone. Each was carved from granite to symbolize incidents on the field that day.

Positioned on the extreme left of the Union line west of Gettysburg, the 121st Pennsylvania witnessed numbers of shells bursting all around them that afternoon. The men held out against tremendous pressure from the Confederate units on the field. Under intense fire, their flag was shot to pieces and the staff broken. Eventually the line here was broken and the 121st was forced back through the town to Cemetery Hill. Along the way the Color Sergeant, William Hardy, stopped to pick up a roofing shingle lying in the street. He later used it to splice the shattered shaft of the flag pole together. For the remainder of the war the repaired flag staff served as a reminder of the intense shelling and musketry fire the unit experienced here at Gettysburg that day.

KLS

LOCATION: DOUBLEDAY AVENUE
DEDICATED: SEPTEMBER 11, 1889
COST: $1500
DESIGNER/CONTRACTOR: HEIMS AND BYE
MATERIAL: QUINCY GRANITE

SECTION TWO: THE CONFEDERATE BATTLELINE

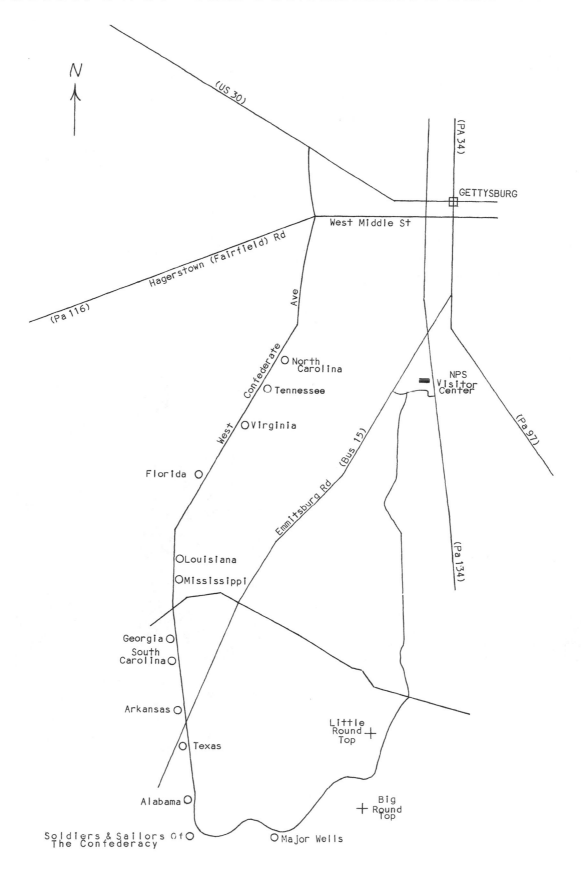

North Carolina State Memorial

To compensate for the lack of southern regimental monuments on the field, over the last seventy years, the various southern states have placed large memorials along the Seminary Ridge battle line. One of the earliest of these was the North Carolina Memorial built to honor twenty-three infantry regiments, three cavalry regiments, three artillery batteries and one infantry battalion that participated in the battle. The statue was sculpted by Gutzon Borglum whose works included the carving of the Presidents at Mt. Rushmore. Among the most artistic monuments on the field, it was designed to commemorate the valor, bravery, and courage of the men from North Carolina.[1]

Located approximately where Pettigrew's North Carolina Brigade of Heth's division emerged into the open fields during Pickett's Charge, Borglum wanted to depict a group of infantrymen who had " . . . just been ordered to charge across that very bloody battlefield."[2] One figure represents a wounded officer who is urging his men on, pointing out the enemy to the front. To his rear, a veteran whispers words of encouragement to a younger comrade while behind the group the colorbearer brings up their flag.[3] All of the faces of the men were modeled using photographs of actual Confederate veterans. The model for the color bearer was Orren Randolph Smith of Henderson, North Carolina, the man who had designed the Confederate national flag, the "Stars and Bars."[4]

Near the main statue is a monolith containing the names of the North Carolina units that were a part of the Army of Northern Virginia. It was built under the auspices of the North Carolina division of the United Daughters of the Confederacy and was dedicated the same day as the main statue.

[1] Craven, *Sculptures at Gettysburg*, p. 86

[2] William C. Davis, *Gettysburg: The Story Behind the Scenery*, (Las Vegas: K. C. Publications, Inc., 1983), p. 37; Craven, *Sculptures*, p. 86.

[3] Herbert L. Grimm and Paul L. Roy, *Human Interest Stories of the Three Days Battles at Gettysburg with Pictures*, (Gettysburg: Times and News Publishing Company, 1969), p. 50.

[4] Craven, *Sculptures*, p. 86

LOCATION: WEST CONFEDERATE AVENUE
DEDICATED: JULY 3, 1929
COST: $50,000
SCULPTOR: GUTZON BORGLUM
CONTRACTOR: A. KUNST FOUNDRY
MATERIAL: STANDARD BRONZE
SPECIFICATIONS: HT—15'9"
                   BASE—6'6"W × 9'9"L

LS

Tennessee State Memorial

Tennessee was the last of the southern states represented in the battle of Gettysburg to place a monument on the field. It is the only state memorial built exclusively through the use of private contributions.[1] On the face of the stone is an etching of three soldiers representing each of the Tennessee regiments in the battle. Three gray, marble stars are on top of the die symbolizing divisions of the state: eastern, central, and western Tennessee. The base is sixteen feet long as Tennessee was the sixteenth state to enter the union. An additional feature is the outline of the state cut into the base.

The units honored by the memorial were part of General Archer's brigade of General Heth's division, the unit that opened the battle for the Confederates on the morning of July 1. The first Confederate ca-

sualty of the battle, Private Henry C. Rison was a member of Company B, 7th Tennessee Infantry. He received a gunshot wound that fractured his thigh while on skirmish duty early on July 1. On August 15, Private Rison died, in a Union hospital. At 3 P.M. on July 3, the survivors of the three Tennessee regiments would participate in the last infantry action of the battle as they advanced from the area near this site to assault the Union lines during "Pickett's Charge". It can therefore be said that Tennessee troops both opened and closed one of the great battles of history.

[1] David G. Martin, *Confederate Monuments at Gettysburg,* (Hightstown, N.J.: Longstreet House, 1986), pp. 50–51.

LS

LOCATION: WEST CONFEDERATE AVENUE
DEDICATED: JULY 2, 1982
COST: $25,000
MATERIAL: CARNELIAN SELECT GRANITE
        ELBERTON GRAY MARBLE
SPECIFICATIONS: 8'10"L × 6'H × 10"W

Virginia State Memorial

The Virginia Memorial was the first of the southern state monuments to be placed at Gettysburg. Its dedication in the summer of 1917 marked the culmination of a decade of efforts to erect a suitable monument to honor the soldiers of the state. Designed and sculpted by Frederick Sievers, the monument effectively combines the honoring of Virginia's soldiers, and the south's great general, Robert E. Lee.[1]

Placed on the site from which Lee observed portions of the battle, the equestrian statue of the General ranks among the finest anywhere in the world. To capture the features, Sievers studied photographs and life masks of Lee done shortly before the General's death in 1870.[2] Personal acquaintances who viewed the finished work felt that it was the best likeness ever executed.[3] To capture the essence of Lee's mount, the sculptor travelled to Lexington, Virginia to study the skeleton of Traveller, on display at Washington and Lee University. A live horse, closely matching the size, shape, and bearing of Traveller was used as the actual model.

Contrasting with the quiet calm of Lee is the action filled grouping at the base, portraying the typical Confederate soldier. The seven figures were to represent all of the diverse elements that made up the Army of Northern Virginia. Of the seven, the artillery bugler and the cavalry colorbearer are both boys, as many who served in that war on both sides were young. The remaining five represent individuals from all walks of life. The soldier on the left, "tearing cartridge" in preparation of loading, was a professional man in civilian life. Next to him, holding the musket with fixed bayonet, a mechanic. A former artist-turned-soldier stands beneath the horse firing a pistol while nearby a businessman-soldier swings his musket to ward off the advancing foe. The soldier standing beside the bugler represents the farmer, a background which many of the soldiers, North and South, had in common. Sievers sculpted all as robust men to symbolize the vigor of the Army of Northern Virginia. The debris of battle, so vividly seen strewn around the base of the figures, is symbolic of the struggle in which Virginia's citizen-soldiers fought so gallantly.[4]

[1] See Craven, *Sculptures at Gettysburg*, p. 85; Davis, *Story Behind the Scenery*, p. 36.
[2] Craven, *Sculptures at Gettysburg*, p. 82.
[3] Grimm and Roy, *Human Interest Stories*, p. 16.
[4] N. A. Meligakes, *The Spirit of Gettysburg*, (Gettysburg: The Bookmark, 1950), p. 175.

LOCATION: WEST CONFEDERATE AVENUE
DEDICATED: JUNE 8, 1917
COST: $50,000
SCULPTOR: FREDERICK WILLIAM SIEVERS
CONTRACTOR; BASE–VAN AMRINGE GRANITE
     CO.
     STATUES–TIFFANY STUDIO
MATERIAL: WESTERLY GRANITE
     STANDARD BRONZE
SPECIFICATIONS: BASE–28'W × 32'6.5"L
     PEDESTAL–10'W × 13'7"L × 24'H
     TOTAL HEIGHT–41'
     SOLDIERS–5'W × 18'L × 16'H
     LEE & TRAVELLER–14'H

FWH

Florida State Memorial

Florida was represented by three small regiments in the battle of Gettysburg and their services are honored and commemorated by the Florida State Memorial. Located in the general area where Brigadier General Edward A. Perry's Florida brigade, under the temporary command of Colonel David Lang, was located during the battle, the monument consists of two granite plinths. The smaller plinth contains an inscription beneath three stars. These stars represent the 2nd, 5th, and 8th Florida Infantry Regiments. The sole decoration on the larger plinth is the state seal of Florida. The memorial was dedicated on the one-hundredth anniversary of the battle, July 3, 1963.

LS

LOCATION: WEST CONFEDERATE AVENUE
DEDICATED: JULY 3, 1963
COST: $20,000
DESIGNER: J. B. HILL
CONTRACTOR: BRUNS MEMORIAL COMPANY
MATERIAL: SELECT SOUTHERN GRANITE
SPECIFICATIONS: BASE—11'8"L × 4'6"W
                       HEIGHT—14'3"
                       PLINTH—4'8"H × 1'6"W
                       PLINTH—4'6"H × 1'5"W

Louisiana State Memorial

The erection of the Louisiana State Memorial, one of the more recent on the field, culminated a movement begun by the Louisiana Division of the United Daughters of the Confederacy in 1966. One of the three southern state monuments designed and sculpted by Donald DeLue, this one consists of a bronze statue of two figures. The first, a nine-foot long, reclining artilleryman represents a member of the Washington Artillery of New Orleans. Fallen, perhaps mortally wounded, a comrade covered his chest with a Confederate battle flag which the dying man has clutched to his heart. The second figure, a ten-foot tall female represents the "Spirit of the Confederacy" soaring over her dead soldiers.[1] A dove of peace is nestled in the reeds beneath the woman.

In her right hand held aloft is the flaming cannonball symbolic of ordnance and artillery. This perhaps lends greater credence to a variant explanation of the soaring figure. It has often been said that it represents St. Barbara, the patron-saint of artillerymen. She was a woman who lived in Asia Minor about 300 A.D., the daughter of a very wealthy man. Her conversion to Christianity infuriated her father who promptly took her before the province's prefect for judgment. There she was condemned to death by beheading, her own father carrying out the sentence. As he returned home after the execution, the legend states that he was struck by a lightning bolt which consumed his body. Because of the fate befalling her executioner, Barbara came to be regarded as the patron to be called upon to protect one in a storm. Gunpowder's invention, and the frequent accidental explosions that resulted from its use, led to St. Barbara gaining the additional role as the artilleryman's patron.[2]

[1] Martin, *Confederate Monuments*, pp. 41–42.
[2] United States Field Artillery Association, Ft. Sill, Oklahoma; Bernard and Fawn Brodie, *From Crossbow to H-Bomb*, (New York: Dell Publishing Co., Inc., 1962), p. 49.

LOCATION: WEST CONFEDERATE AVENUE
DEDICATED: JUNE 11, 1971
COST: $100,000
SCULPTOR: DONALD DELUE
CONTRACTOR: CAST IN ITALY
MATERIAL: POLISHED GREEN GRANITE
              BRONZE
SPECIFICATIONS: BASE–9'10"SQ × 3'H
              OVERALL HT–22'

FWH

Mississippi State Memorial

The third southern monument on the field attributed to sculptor Donald DeLue is the Mississippi Memorial, erected on the site where General William Barksdale's Mississippi brigade waited before going into battle the evening of July 2. Built to honor eleven infantry regiments, one infantry battalion, one cavalry regiment, and one artillery battery from Mississippi, the monument illustrates the bravery, devotion, and sacrifice of the Mississippi soldier in the face of great odds.

The statue represents two infantrymen of Barksdale's brigade in their advance across the Sherfy and Trostle farms. In the fierce fighting which will eventually overwhelm the Union line along the Emmitsburg Road, one has fallen mortally wounded. His comrade has stopped beside him and using his musket as a club, defends the fallen flag. In the close hand-to-hand fighting that often characterized the battle on July 2, this scene may have been witnessed many times.[1]

[1] Craven, *Sculptures at Gettysburg*, p. 90.

DWM

LOCATION: WEST CONFEDERATE AVENUE
DEDICATED: OCTOBER 19, 1973
COST: $100,000
SCULPTOR: DONALD DELUE
CONTRACTOR: CAST IN ITALY
MATERIAL: LAC DUBONNET GRANITE
          BRONZE
SPECIFICATIONS: BASE—7'11"L × 3'11"W
          HEIGHT—16'2"

Georgia State Memorial

As the centennial celebration of the Civil War approached in the spring of 1961, the Georgia legislature appropriated money to construct memorials to honor all Georgians, specifically those numbered as casualties in the battles of Gettysburg and Antietam. In September of that year, two identical monuments were dedicated, one on each field. Erected near where General Paul Semmes' Georgia brigade was in position, the simple shaft of Georgia blue granite is adorned with the state seal of Georgia front and back. The only inscription is a simple epitaph to the Georgia dead:

> We Sleep Here in Obedience to Law
> When Duty Called, We Came
> When Country Called, We Died

LS

LOCATION: WEST CONFEDERATE AVENUE
DEDICATED: SEPTEMBER 21, 1961
DESIGNER: HARRY SELLERS
CONTRACTOR: MARIETTA MEMORIALS
MATERIAL: GEORGIA BLUE GRANITE
SPECIFICATIONS: BASE–7'7"SQ
SHAFT–3'SQ × 15'6"H

South Carolina State Memorial

The South Carolina State Memorial at Gettysburg was erected in 1963 under the auspices of the state's Civil War Centennial Commission. Designed to honor the eleven state infantry regiments, two cavalry regiments, and the five artillery battalions, the monument was located where General J. B. Kershaw's South Carolina brigade formed up for the advance against the Union positions on July 2.

Symbolically there are several features on the monument that clearly tie it to South Carolina, the most prominent feature being the state outline and seal carved into the main shaft. On each side of the monument is a stone with a carved palmetto tree which underscores the nickname of "Palmetto State". The side dies detail the names and assignments of each South Carolina unit in the Army of Northern Virginia.

At the bottom of the base is an excerpt from a song "Ode at Magnolia Cemetery" sung during ceremonies decorating graves of the Confederate dead on Confederate Memorial Day in April, 1867. "There is no holier spot of ground than where defeated valor lies, by mourning beauty crowned." This was written by Henry Timrod, a native of Charleston. Active during the Civil War, and up until his death in 1867, Timrod wrote on southern themes. His poems were so well known throughout the south that he received the title "Poet Laureate of the Confederacy." The line was quite appropriate to this field and was therefore included on the monument.

FWH

LOCATION: WEST CONFEDERATE AVENUE
DEDICATED: JULY 2, 1963
COST: $15,000
DESIGNER: J. B. HILL
CONTRACTOR: BRUNS MONUMENT COMPANY
MATERIAL: WINBORO BLUE GRANITE
SPECIFICATIONS: BASE–23′L × 3′9″W
CENTRAL PLINTH–5′5″L ×
2′6″W × 14′2″H

Arkansas State Memorial

The state memorial of Arkansas, erected shortly after the close of the Civil War Centennial, honors the only regiment of that state to participate in the battle of Gettysburg. Part of Robertson's Texas brigade, the 3rd Arkansas Infantry, formed up for the assaults on the Union line at this location. The die of the monument contains an outline of the state of Arkansas flanked on both sides by a lightly carved bas relief of advancing infantrymen. At the corners of the monument, two-foot square aluminum blocks were placed, with each having a Confederate battle flag carved on the faces. A rather unusual metal to find in a monument, it was intended to represent Arkansas' modern day role as a prominent aluminum producing state.[1]

[1] Martin, *Confederate Monuments*, pp. 36.

LS

LOCATION: WEST CONFEDERATE AVENUE
DEDICATED: JUNE 18, 1966
COST: $50,000
CONTRACTOR: COBB MEMORIAL COMPANY
MATERIAL: MT. AIRY GRANITE
SPECIFICATIONS: 28'L × 8'W × 8'6"H

Texas State Memorial

One of the best fighting units of the Army of Northern Virginia was John Bell Hood's Texas brigade consisting of the 1st, 4th, and 5th Texas regiments. Historian Harold B. Simpson, of the Texas State Civil War Centennial Commission, noted that despite the fame of the unit, only two small monuments, one near the present state memorial, and the other at the Wilderness battlefield, had been erected to honor the unit. The one here at Gettysburg, located a short distance away, had been placed here in 1913, not by a veteran's group, but through the efforts of a group of private citizens.[1]

The decision to place a state sponsored monument here was tied to an appropriation to erect identical monuments on eleven battlefields where Texas troops had fought.[2] Those at Antietam and the Wilderness, along with the one at Gettysburg, specifically honor the old Texas brigade. Constructed of Texas Red Granite, the monument's only adornment is the lone star of Texas placed near the top. This simple monument appears plain when compared with the other southern state monuments, but the fact that identical monuments exist on other fields serves to assure that the sacrifice of Texas soldiers on one battlefield was not made to appear any greater or less on any specific field.

[1] Martin, *Confederate Monuments*, pp. 133.

[2] The eleven sites are: Antietam, Wilderness, Gettysburg, Bentonville, Chickamauga, Ft. Donelson, Kennesaw Mountain, Mansfield, Pea Ridge, Shiloh, Anthony, Texas. The only large scale monument specifically erected to honor all Confederate soldiers from Texas, was built at Vicksburg.

DWM

LOCATION: SOUTH CONFEDERATE AVENUE
DEDICATED: SEPTEMBER 1964
COST: $1,000
DESIGNER: HAROLD B. SIMPSON
CONTRACTOR: STASSWENDER MARBLE & GRANITE WORKS
MATERIAL: TEXAS RED GRANITE
SPECIFICATIONS: BASE–3'6"L × 2'6"H
SHAFT–2'7"L × 1'W × 7'8"H

Alabama State Memorial

Alabama was the third southern state to erect a state memorial on the field at Gettysburg. Inspired by the Alabama Division of the United Daughters of the Confederacy, funds were approved out of state revenues in 1927. The memorial was designed to honor the gallantry and sacrifice of Alabama soldiers who served here. General Evander Law's Alabama brigade, positioned on the extreme right of the Army of Northern Virginia, was centered about where the monument now stands.

The central figure of the sculpture represents the spirit of Alabama.[1] The two soldiers on either side symbolize the "Spirit" and the "Determination" of all Alabama soldiers.[2] On the left, the wounded figure is being comforted by the female figure at the same time she urges the other soldier on. To indicate the continuance of the struggle, an ammunition pouch is being passed on to the soldier continuing the fight. The monument was dedicated in November, 1933, seventy years after the battle.

[1] See Craven, *Sculptures at Gettysburg*, p. 94; A variation of this is that the figure represents the "Spirit of the Confederacy": Gilbert, *The Blue and the Gray*, p. 55.

[2] Gilbert, *The Blue and the Gray*, p. 55.

LS

LOCATION: SOUTH CONFEDERATE AVENUE
DEDICATED: NOVEMBER 12, 1933
COST: $12,000
SCULPTOR: JOSEPH W. URNER
DESIGNER/CONTRACTOR: HAMMAKER BROTHERS
BRONZE: ROMAN BRONZE COMPANY
MATERIAL: VERMONT GRANITE
STANDARD BRONZE
SPECIFICATIONS: OVERALL–19'L × 8'3"W × 12'H
TOTAL WEIGHT–28 TONS

The Soldiers and Sailors of the Confederacy Memorial

As the Civil War Centennial drew to a close in the 1960's, a movement was underway to erect a monument to honor the valor of all members of the Confederate armies and navies. It was decided that Gettysburg, as the greatest battle of that war and the symbolic "High Water Mark" of the Confederacy, would be the ideal location for such a monument. Contributions were received from all eleven states that had formed the Confederacy and from three former border states, Missouri, Maryland, and Kentucky.

Sculpted by Donald DeLue, the statue represents a charging southern color bearer, urging his comrades to follow him. The pink granite base contains the names of each of the states that contributed

soldiers to the Confederate army. At the rear of the base is engraved the name Walter Washington Williams who served as a forage master with a Texas regiment during the war. On December 19, 1959, at the age of one hundred and seventeen years, one month, and five days, Williams died. The last member of the armed forces of the Confederate States of America had finally joined his comrades.[1]

[1] There has been some controversy in the past over the validity of Walter Williams status as the "last" veteran. NPS officials currently doubt the claim, feeling that John B. Salling, a veteran of Company D of the 25th Virginia Infantry, rightfully deserves the honor. Salling died March 16, 1959 at the age of one hundred and twelve years, ten months, and one day.

LS

LOCATION: SOUTH CONFEDERATE AVENUE
DEDICATED: AUGUST 25, 1965
SCULPTOR: DONALD DELUE
ARCHITECT: HENRY DACY
MATERIAL: PINK GRANITE
              STANDARD BRONZE
SPECIFICATIONS: HEIGHT—19'3"
                  CIRCUMFERENCE—12'

William Wells Portrait Statue

On July 3, 1863, at 5:00 P.M., the fighting in the battle of Gettysburg was essentially over. On the extreme Union left, one small act remained to be performed. General Elon J. Farnsworth, accompanied by four companies of the 1st Vermont Cavalry under the command of Major William Wells, charged five Confederate regiments of Law's Alabama brigade. Under heavy musketry and artillery fire the detachment broke into the rear of the Confederate lines near the site of the 1st Vermont's regimental monument. Eventually they turned back to where the charge began, having lost Farnsworth and seventy-five of the two hundred twenty-five troopers that followed him. Major Wells was numbered among the survivors; he would ultimately be awarded a Congressional Medal of Honor for " . . . most distinguished gallantry" in the futile charge.

Wells was one of the best officers produced by the state of Vermont during the war. Enlisting as a private in 1861, he rose to the rank of Brevet Major General by war's end, having received more promotions than any other Vermont officer during the war.[1] To honor his memory and the memory of the men under his command, Vermont appropriated $6,000 for use in erecting a portrait statue on the site where his detachment began their fateful charge that day. The sculptor, J. Otto Schweizer, used a variety of Wells' possessions to insure the accuracy of the statue. The uniform, hat, boots, belt, and revolver actually used by the General during the war were loaned to Schweizer to model from.[2] To capture the facial features, Schweizer used a photograph of Wells taken during the war. Friends of the General were so pleased with the sculptor's work that an exact copy was ordered and erected the following year at Battery Park in Burlington, Vermont.

The statue was also intended to honor the men of the 1st Vermont Cavalry who participated in the charge. To accomplish this an additional $2,000 was donated by the Survivor's Association to place a bronze battle scene on the face of the boulder that served as the statue's base. The sculptor's desire for accuracy led him to model each of the faces visible in the plaque from photographs provided of the actual participants. The horses depicted are a breed known as "Morgan," the same type on which the unit was mounted when they left Vermont for the front in 1861.[3] Out in front, Major Wells is depicted with a raised sabre while General Farnsworth falls mortally wounded at his side. Nearly twenty additional figures on the plaque are identified by name.

[1] H. Nelson Jackson, Compiler, *In Affectionate Memory of Major-General William Wells: Dedication of the Statue to Brevet Major-General William Wells and the officers and men of the First Regiment Vermont Cavalry on the Battlefield of Gettysburg, July 3, 1913*, (Privately published, 1914), p. 201.
[2] Ibid., pp. 65–67.
[3] Ibid., p. 47.

LOCATION: SOUTH CONFEDERATE AVENUE
DEDICATED: JULY 3, 1913
COST: $8000
SCULPTOR: J. OTTO SCHWEIZER
CONTRACTOR: VAN AMRINGE GRANITE
            COMPANY
MATERIAL: STANDARD BRONZE
SPECIFICATIONS: HT–8'

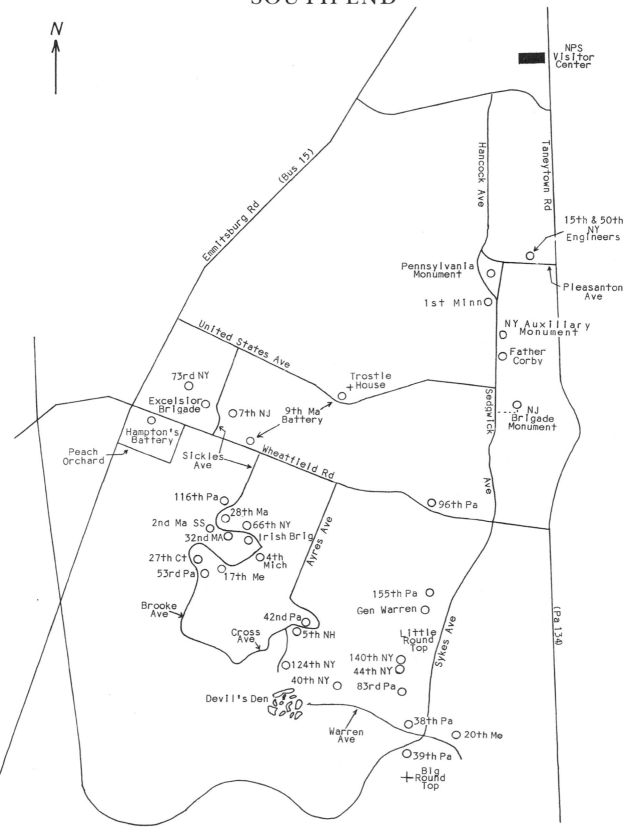

N

NPS Visitor Center

Hancock Ave

Taneytown Rd

Emmitsburg Rd (Bus 15)

15th & 50th NY Engineers

Pennsylvania Monument

Pleasanton Ave

1st Minn

NY Auxiliary Monument

United States Ave

Father Corby

73rd NY

Trostle House

Sedgwick Ave

NJ Brigade Monument

Excelsior Brigade

7th NJ

9th Ma Battery

Hampton's Battery

Peach Orchard

Sickles Ave

Wheatfield Rd

116th Pa

96th Pa

28th Ma

2nd Ma SS

66th NY

Ayres Ave

32nd MA

Irish Brig

27th Ct

4th Mich

53rd Pa

17th Me

155th Pa

Gen Warren

Brooke Ave

42nd Pa

Cross Ave

5th NH

Little Round Top

Sykes Ave

124th NY

140th NY

44th NY

40th NY

83rd Pa

Devil's Den

Warren Ave

38th Pa

20th Me

39th Pa

Big Round Top

(Pa 134)

39th Pennsylvania Infantry (10th Pennsylvania Reserves)

The 39th Pennsylvania Infantry was one of the thirteen complete infantry regiments organized, trained, and equipped at the expense of the state of Pennsylvania. Raised by order of Governor Andrew Curtin, these regiments were designated the Pennsylvania Reserve Corps. Nine of these regiments participated in the battle of Gettysburg as part of the Pennsylvania Reserve Division of the 5th Corps.[1]

The monument of the 39th Pennsylvania, more commonly known as the 10th Reserves, was cast entirely of bronze. The unit was sent into this area after the close of the fighting on the evening of July 2 to aid in securing and holding the position against any future Confederate assaults. The Veteran's Association of the 10th Reserve chose to design a statue that would depict the duties the regiment performed here. It represents a skirmisher in the position of "trail arms" climbing the ". . . rugged, stormy heights of Round Top."[2] He is depicted half stooping and bending forward to give the appearance of the advance up the slope. His eyes eternally gaze ahead, looking through the trees for signs of the long departed enemy.

[1] Patricia L. Faust, ed., *Historical Times Illustrated Encyclopedia of the Civil War,* (New York: Harper and Row, 1986), p. 572–573.

[2] PaMC, Records pertaining to the 39th Pennsylvania Monument.

FWH

LOCATION: SOUTH CONFEDERATE AVENUE
DEDICATED: SEPTEMBER 1890
COST: $3000
DESIGNED: J. H. BUCK
CONTRACTOR: GORHAM MANUFACTURING
     COMPANY
MATERIAL: STANDARD BRONZE
SPECIFICATIONS: PEDESTAL–8'HT
     STATUE–7'HT
     BRONZE 8 PTS COPPER/2 PTS
     TIN

38th Pennsylvania Infantry (9th Pennsylvania Reserves)

The monument to another of the Pennsylvania Reserve regiments, the 38th Pennsylvania Infantry, stands atop a boulder on the position the 9th Reserves held from late evening of July 2 until the close of the battle. On the face of the stone, a bas relief carving of a soldier looks down on the grave of a friend. Entitled "By a Comrades Grave", the monument was designed to commemorate the great sacrifices made by the men of the 9th Reserves throughout the war.[1] The grave on the stone is symbolic of the graves of the unit's men who died in defense of the Union, not just here at Gettysburg, but on many fields on which the regiment had fought.[2]

[1] *Pennsylvania at Gettysburg*, 1:242.
[2] Ibid.

KLS

LOCATION: WARREN AVENUE
DEDICATED: SEPTEMBER 20, 1888 (COMPLETED)
COST: $2450
DESIGNER/CONTRACTOR: SMITH GRANITE
       COMPANY
MATERIAL: BLUE WESTERLY GRANITE
SPECIFICATIONS: 1ST BASE–6'9" × 3'1"
      2ND BASE–5'8" × 2'9"
      TABLET–5'11" × 2'
      TOTAL HEIGHT–11'6"

20th Maine Infantry

The 20th Maine Infantry was the regiment holding the extreme left flank of the Union battle line on the evening of July 2, 1863. Its Colonel, Joshua Chamberlain, had been given orders to hold the position at all costs: to retreat would mean jeopardizing the safety of the rest of the Army of the Potomac. The men quickly came into position overlooking a small ravine that separated the two Round Tops. One company was sent off into the woods to the east to guard against flank attacks.[1]

The Confederate attack swept over the slope of Big Round Top and hit the men of the 20th Maine. Chamberlain's soldiers held tenaciously to their little ledge of rocks repelling assault after assault. One

image that remained burned in Chamberlain's memory of that fight centered around the regimental flag. The color company has sustained heavy casualties and the acrid battle smoke often obscured the flag. Briefly, the smoke-cloud cleared and the Colonel and many of his men were stirred by the sight of Color Sergeant Andrew Tozier standing on the boulder alone, seemingly above the fury of the battle, the flag staff planted at his feet. Holding the flag erect against his body, his arms were free to fire a rifle. There he stood, assisting his comrades in the defense of their line. Eventually ammunition began to run low and Chamberlain was faced with a difficult choice. To stay in position invited disaster; the lack of sufficient cartridges would mean certain defeat. Retreat was out of the question leaving only the possibility of attack as an appropriate option. As yet another Confederate attack appeared eminent, the men were ordered to fix bayonets and on command, the attacked became the attackers. The men of the 20th Maine swept down through the little valley driving the Confederates out of the area and securing the army's flank. On the slope of the little hill they had defended lay the bodies of dozens of their dead and wounded comrades.

In 1886, the survivors of the 20th Maine privately erected the monument on the boulder where Sergeant Tozier held the flag. A small marker several hundred yards away marks the spot where Company B, alone and unsupported, had fought. The main monument was dedicated to the memory of thirty-eight of their comrades who gave their lives that evening. All of their names appear on the monument today.

[1] Maine Gettysburg Monuments Commission, *Maine at Gettysburg: Report of the Maine Commissioners Prepared by the Executive Committee,* (Portland: The Lakeside Press, 1898), p. 259.

LOCATION: WRIGHT AVENUE
DEDICATED: OCTOBER 3, 1886
CONTRACTOR: HALLOWELL GRANITE WORKS
MATERIAL: HALLOWELL GRANITE
SPECIFICATIONS: 4'SQ × 5'4"H

KLS

83rd Pennsylvania Infantry

The 83rd Pennsylvania Infantry, like her sister regiment, the 20th Maine, was part of the 3rd Brigade, 1st Division, 5th Army Corps. Arriving at Little Round Top just minutes before the hill was stormed by Alabama and Texas soldiers, the 83rd was placed in position of the south slope of the hill. Here they struggled valiantly throughout the fight to stem the tide of the Confederate attack. Many members of the 83rd fell as casualties in that conflict. Perhaps the casualty that affected the men greatest was the loss of their former regimental commander, Colonel Strong Vincent, then serving as brigade commander. Colonel Vincent was mortally wounded at the height of the battle as he rushed off to bolster the right end of his line, which began to give away under heavy pressure.

The statue atop the monument officially represents ". . . the figure of a Union officer." Although nothing was ever carved on the monument to indicate the officer's identity, it is Strong Vincent. The Pennsylvania State Monuments Commission, formed to oversee the expenditure of state funds in building the monuments, refused to allow any personal statements or inscriptions on any memorial built under their supervision. This was justified by stating that the monuments were to commemorate the common deeds of the Pennsylvania soldier, not the personal actions of individuals.[1] Even without identification, the old veterans of Vincent's brigade recognized the exceptional likeness of their old commander who, like many others, had paid the supreme price to hold this small piece of landscape.

[1] *Pennsylvania at Gettysburg*, 1:464.

REF

LOCATION: SYKES AVENUE
DEDICATED: SEPTEMBER 11, 1889
COST: $2860
CONTRACTOR: BASE—FREDERICK AND FIELD
  STATUE—BUREAU BROTHERS
MATERIAL: QUINCY GRANITE
  STANDARD BRONZE
SPECIFICATIONS: BASE—8'L × 5'5"W
  OVERALL HEIGHT—18'6"
  STATUE HEIGHT—7'3"

Colonel Strong Vincent   REGIMENTAL HISTORY

44th New York Infantry

By far the largest and most expensive regimental monument on the battlefield today is the massive granite castle honoring the officers and men of the 44th New York Infantry and two companies of the 12th New York Infantry. New York passed an appropriation of $1500 for each regiment designated for monument construction. Friends and regimental survivors supplemented this amount with an additional $9000. Designed by Daniel Butterfield, a former regimental commander of the 12th and the first brigade commander of the 44th, the monument's dimensions were deliberately designed to reflect the units numeric designations. The tower of the castle is forty-four feet high to represent the 44th Infantry, while the interior chamber was laid out to be twelve feet square to honor the 12th Infantry. A

circular staircase inside leads up to an observation deck. Inside the chamber, bronze plaques contain a complete muster roll for each company of the regiment. Two additional plaques contain bas reliefs of two former officers, General Francis Barlow and General Butterfield. Both were present in other capacities at Gettysburg. Barlow was severely wounded north of the town while commanding a division in the 11th Corps, July 1. Butterfield, also known as the composer of the bugle call "Taps", served as the army Chief of Staff at Gettysburg.

The uniqueness of the massive monument of the 44th was matched by that of the regiment itself. The unit was raised as a memorial to Ephraim Elmer Ellsworth, the first Union officer to be killed during the war. Ellsworth had organized a militia unit, the United States Zouave Corps, in 1859. Many of the officers of the 44th served in this unit. An active supporter of Abraham Lincoln during the presidential campaign in 1860, Ellsworth was a personal friend of the new president. At the outbreak of the war he headed for New York where, within forty-eight hours, he had raised a regiment of 2300 men. Shortly after arriving in Washington, his unit was ordered to cross the Potomac river and occupy Alexandria, Virginia. Upon arriving, Ellsworth spotted a Confederate flag flying from the roof of the Marshall House Hotel. He ran up personally and tore the flag down. Coming back down the hotel's proprietor confronted Ellsworth on one of the landings and shot and killed him.

LS

LOCATION: SUMMIT, LITTLE ROUND TOP
DEDICATED: JULY 3, 1893
COST: $10,965
DESIGNER: DANIEL BUTTERFIELD
CONTRACTOR: GEORGE H. MITCHELL
MATERIAL: PROSPECT HILL, MAINE GRANITE
           STANDARD BRONZE
SPECIFICATIONS: OVERALL LENGTH–28'0"
           OVERALL WIDTH–21'8"
           OVERALL HEIGHT–44'
           INTERIOR CHAMBER–12'SQ ×
             12'H
           INTERIOR TABLETS–1'9" × 3'7"
           INTERIOR TOWER–6'DIA
           EXTERIOR TABLETS–2'8" × 2'4"

As Ellsworth's body lay in state at Albany, a group of citizens laid the foundations to raise a unit to be called the "People's Ellsworth Regiment" or "Ellsworth's Avengers". The idea developed to take one man from each town and ward in the state. Each had to be able-bodied, temperate, moral, unmarried, five-feet eight-inches or taller, and no older than thirty. When accepted, the recruit was required to pay twenty dollars to the regimental fund.[1] Although never quite fulfilling the goal of total state representation, the unique makeup of the 44th New York, and its contributions in battle, earned it a reputation matched by the size of its monument.

[1] E. A. Nash, *History of the Forty-Fourth Regiment New York Volunteer Infantry in the Civil War, 1861–1865*, (Chicago: R. R. Donnelley and Sons, 1911), pp. 8–9; New York Monuments Commission for the Battlefields of Gettysburg and Chattanooga, *New York at Gettysburg: The Final Report on the Battlefield at Gettysburg*, 3 vols. (Albany: J. B. Lyon Company, Printers, 1902), 1:360, 367.

140th New York Infantry

Overshadowed and overlooked due to its proximity to the 44th New York "castle," the small monument to the 140th New York Infantry honors a unit that was instrumental in saving Little Round Top during the Confederate assault on July 2. As General Evander Law's Alabamians stormed the south slope of the hill, defended by the 20th Maine, 83rd Pennsylvania, and 44th New York, two regiments of Texas Infantry slipped into the valley below and partially flanked the remaining regiment of Vincent's brigade . . . the 16th Michigan. The right flank companies of that regiment began to give way under the pressure. At that moment, reinforcements in the form of the 140th New York arrived at the summit. Their commander, Colonel Patrick O'Rorke, had graduated first in his class at West Point just two years before. With no time available to load muskets, bayonets were fixed and the unit went in to bolster the crumbling line. The Confederates were thrown back down the hill and the position was secured. Colonel O'Rorke lay dead approximately where the monument is now located having been shot through the neck during the charge.[1] The Veteran's Association of the 140th New York designed the monument as a memorial to all from the unit who died at Gettysburg. Centered on the front of the die is a bronze bust of Colonel O'Rorke, placed there by the unanimous wish of the surviving comrades who had followed him into battle.[2]

[1] *New York at Gettysburg*, 3:958.
[2] Ibid.

LOCATION: SUMMIT OF LITTLE ROUND TOP
DEDICATED: SEPTEMBER 17, 1889
COST: $1500
SCULPTOR: J. G. HAMILTON
DESIGNER/CONTRACTOR: SMITH GRANITE
                          COMPANY
MATERIAL: WESTERLY GRANITE
          STANDARD BRONZE
SPECIFICATIONS: BASE–7'0"L × 5'8"W × 7'3"H
          MEDALLION–2'2"DIA
          TABLETS–1'4" × 2'0"

FWH

Gouverneur Warren Portrait Statue

The portrait statue of General Gouverneur K. Warren, Chief Engineer of the Army of the Potomac, stands on the boulder from which he spotted the Confederate advance on Little Round Top the afternoon of July 2. Following the controversial repositioning of General Daniel Sickles 3rd Corps, this hill was left essentially unoccupied. Only a small group of signalmen remained behind and they were packing up in preparation of leaving. As Warren surveyed the region south and west of the hill he caught a glimpse of the Confederate battlelines forming on Warfield and Seminary Ridges. Ordering the signalmen to remain to give the appearance of occupation, Warren sent his aides out to locate reinforcements to rush to the hill. His prompt action allowed the hill to remain in Union hands earning him the praise "Savior of Little Round Top".

Twenty-three years after Warren's services on this field, the Veteran's Association of his first command, the 5th New York Infantry, decided to erect a monument to him. Survivors and other interested individuals were sent printed appeals for money.[1] The efforts were quite successful with all funds necessary having been privately raised. This first statue to a New York commander at Gettysburg was dedicated in 1888.

[1] *New York at Gettysburg*, 3:976, Vanderslice, *Gettysburg Then and Now*, p. 431.

LOCATION: SUMMIT OF LITTLE ROUND TOP
DEDICATED: AUGUST 8, 1888
COST: $5000
SCULPTOR: KARL GERHARDT
CONTRACTOR: HENRY BONNARD BRONZE
                COMPANY
MATERIAL: STANDARD BRONZE
SPECIFICATIONS: HEIGHT 9'
                      WEIGHT 2600 LBS

LS

The monument to the 155th Pennsylvania Infantry stands on the summit of Little Round Top where the regiment waited in position July 2 and July 3. Built by the Veteran's Association using money raised exclusively from friends and veterans in the Pittsburgh area, the monument was dedicated in 1886.[1] It contains a brief history of the unit including a listing of the significant battles in which they participated.

When the state appropriation was granted, the regiment decided to use the money to place a life size marble statue of a private soldier in the zouave uniform that characterized the 155th Pennsylvania. The original Zouaves had been a part of the French army in Algeria in the 1830's. Zouave units were made up of native tribesmen dressed in a uniform of red baggy pants, usually set off with white leggings, a dark blue jacket and a tassled fez for a hat.[2] Known for their ferocity and bravery in battle, the Zouave reputation travelled far, leading to their emulation by the militia units of this country. The uniform you see on the statue differs little from their Algerian predecessors.

A former private in company F of the regiment, Samuel W. Hill was the model for the Zouave atop the monument. Present during the battle, he had been specifically selected by the regiment's design committee to pose for it.[3] It stands, fully armed and equipped, facing the valley where the 155th waited and watched, ready to defend the hill if the Confederates attempted to return.

[1] John T. Porter, *Under the Maltese Cross: Antietam to Appomattox—The Loyal Uprising in Western Pennsylvania 1861–1865*, (Akron, Ohio: The Werner Company, 1910), p. 636–637.
[2] Faust, *Encyclopedia of the Civil War*, p. 850.
[3] Ibid., p. 649.

FWH

LOCATION: SUMMIT OF LITTLE ROUND TOP
DEDICATED: SEPTEMBER 17, 1886 (BASE)
COST: $3,000
DESIGNER/CONTRACTOR: RYEGATE GRANITE
WORKS
MATERIAL: RYEGATE GRANITE (PEDESTAL)
HARDWICK GRANITE (STATUE)

96th Pennsylvania Infantry

The 96th Pennsylvania Infantry played a defensive role in the battle of July 2. Placed in this position during the course of the fight, they would hold it until the army began the pursuit of Lee on July 5. Although involved in no fighting at Gettysburg, they, like other reserve units, remained vigilant and ready to engage the enemy if the need arose. Their monument was designed to reflect the defensive role the unit performed in the battle. The statue of the prone infantryman was the work of a young artisan em-ployed by the contractor.[1] In position watching for signs of the enemy, the infantryman's thumb is on the hammer of the gun prepared to open fire in an instant. Great detail is evident in the sculpture, from the Greek Cross 6th Corps symbol on the crown of the kepi, to the footprint visible to the left of the soldier's foot. This is the type of intricate detail present in many of the monuments of this field.

[1] *Pennsylvania at Gettysburg,* 1:519.

LS

LOCATION: WHEATFIELD ROAD
DEDICATED: JUNE 21, 1888
COST: $1500
SCULPTOR: A. ZELLER
DESIGNER/CONTRACTOR: RICHARD COLLINS
                         GRANITE WORKS,
                         POTTSVILLE, PA.

42nd Pennsylvania Infantry (13th Pennsylvania Reserves)

It could be said of the 42nd Pennsylvania Infantry that they were known by more names than any other unit in the Union army. Aside from the state designation, the 42nd Pennsylvania was also known as the 13th Pennsylvania Reserves, the 1st Rifles, and the Pennsylvania Bucktails. The latter was perhaps the name of which they were proudest. Raised in the spring of 1861, the reputation of the unit's marksmanship spread throughout the army. They adopted the custom of each man wearing on his kepi the tail of a deer he had shot. Their record was such that the Secretary of War Edwin M. Stanton ordered one of the 42nd's officers, Major Roy Stone, to return to Pennsylvania and recruit an entire brigade of Bucktails (149th and 150th Pennsylvania).[1] These regiments adopted the same emblem, causing great bitterness among the members of the 42nd who promptly dubbed the upstarts "Bogus Bucktails." Twenty-five years later, as the monuments to the newer Bucktail units were erected, the bitterness of the original Bucktails bubbled to the surface. They officially protested to the Pennsylvania Monument Commission that they had been authorized by the Secretary of War to wear the bucktail as a distinctive badge. They further argued that no other unit had received the authorization to wear it, to claim the title, or to place either on a monument.[2] Their argument was ignored. When the monument to the 42nd was finally erected by the state of Pennsylvania in 1890 the statue of an infantryman with a bucktailed kepi was placed on top overlooking the scene of conflict. At the bottom of the statue's base, the word "Bucktails" proclaims to future generations the unit's proud association with that unique symbol.

[1] Faust, *Encyclopedia of the Civil War*, p. 573.
[2] PaMC, Letter from William Rauch, Secretary of the Veteran's Association, 13th Reserves, to Board of Commissioners, December 9, 1987.

LS

LOCATION: AYRES AVENUE
DEDICATED: SEPTEMBER 1890
COST: $1500
DESIGNER/CONTRACTOR: SMITH GRANITE COMPANY
MATERIAL: RED WESTERLY GRANITE
SPECIFICATIONS: BASE—3′9″SQ × 4′6″H
STATUE—7′0″

5th New Hampshire Infantry

Inside the woods edging the Wheatfield is the rather odd looking pile of granite boulders that constitutes the monument to the 5th New Hampshire infantry and their former commander, Colonel Edward Cross. The four boulders forming the base, as well as the one on top, were taken from various locations around the battlefield. The octagonal block in the middle is made of New Hampshire granite. The only feature present, aside from the bronze plaques, is the carved trefoil in the top boulder, symbol of the 2nd Army Corps. The monument is placed on the spot, located by a committee of veterans in 1886, where brigade commander Cross was struck and mortally wounded during the battle.[1]

Colonel Cross had already survived twelve woundings in his military career, nine of those since the Civil War began. As he led his brigade into battle that afternoon, the premonition of approaching death apparently hung heavy over Cross. Overdue for promotion to Brigadier General, his Corps commander, Major General Winfield Scott Hancock rode up as Cross's brigade awaited orders. Spotting the Colonel, Hancock said, "Colonel Cross, this day will bring you a star." Cross shook his head and replied "No, General, this is my last battle." Within minutes of this encounter, Caldwell's Division advanced into battle. As Colonel Cross directed the advance of his old unit through the woods edging the Wheatfield, a Confederate soldier, positioned behind a large boulder fifty yards south of the present monument, saw Cross and fired. The Colonel fell with his thirteenth and final wound.[2]

Joining Cross's name on the monument of the 5th New Hampshire are the names of thirty other men who fell with him in the swirling action in and around the Wheatfield that July afternoon. Perhaps the words of the orator during the monument's dedication best sums up the symbolism of the 5th New Hampshire monument: ". . . like the granite boulder we consecrate today were these dead heros, . . . men of the Granite State, hard, enduring, patient, unmovable . . ."[3]

[1] Vanderslice, *Gettysburg Then and Now*, p. 397; William A. Child, *A History of the Fifth Regiment New Hampshire Volunteers in the American Civil War 1861–1865*, (Bristol: R. W. Musgrove, Printer, 1893), p. 226.

[2] Charles A. Hale, "With Colonel Cross in the Wheatfield," *Civil War Times Illustrated*, August 1974, pp. 30–38. The boulder which the Confederate used for cover still exists just southwest of the intersection of Ayres and Sickles Avenues. For a variation to the story see *Pennsylvania at Gettysburg*, 2:628.

[3] Child, *A History of the Fifth New Hampshire*, p. 231.

LOCATION: AYRES AVENUE
DEDICATED: JULY 2, 1886
COST: $600
DESIGNER: MAJOR L. FRED RICE (31ST MASS)
CONTRACTOR: J. FRANK HUNTON, CONCORD, N.H.
MATERIAL: GETTYSBURG GRANITE
CONCORD GRANITE

FWH

124th New York Infantry

The monument to the 124th New York Infantry is the only one on the battlefield that contains a full length portrait statue of a regimental commander— Colonel A. Van Horne Ellis. Recruited in Orange County, New York, it proudly bore the nickname throughout the army "Orange Blossoms." The first monument built to honor a New York regiment, it was paid for from funds raised by the Regimental Association. Much of the money came from citizens of Orange County.[1]

The statue of Colonel Ellis is portrayed as he was supposed to have been standing, arms folded, patiently watching as Robertson's Texas brigade advanced towards his unit's position that afternoon. He would later be killed as the fighting swept over Houck's Ridge. Officers during the Civil War were expected to be calm in battle in order to inspire the men under their command. Exposing themselves recklessly to enemy fire to display bravery was another necessary trait. Understanding these basic qualities of the Civil War officer corps makes it somewhat easier to accept this portrayal of Ellis during those tension filled moments before the fighting commenced. The bronze sash and sword are replacements for vandalism done years ago to the original granite.

[1] Vanderslice, *Gettysburg Then and Now,* p. 368, 424; *New York at Gettysburg,* 2:863–864.

DWM

LOCATION: SICKLES AVENUE AT DEVIL'S DEN
DEDICATED: JULY 2, 1884
COST: $2714
DESIGNER/CONTRACTOR: GRANITE–P. B. LAIRD
                        BRONZE–MAURICE J.
                        POWERS
MATERIAL: ST. JOHNSBURY, VT. GRANITE
               STANDARD BRONZE
SPECIFICATIONS: BASE–4'5"SQ
                    HEIGHT–16'2"
                    STATUE–7'0"
                    FRONT TABLET–2'7" × 3'8"
                    REAR TABLET–2'4" × 3'4"

53rd Pennsylvania Infantry

"... our work here is indeed complete ... the Fifty-Third Pennsylvania, vigilant in its country's cause, will hereafter, even when we may all be sleeping the long sleep, still maintain on permanent post a sentinel ... and by his silent presence keep alive the same self-sacrificing patriotism [the 53rd] displayed."[1]

With these words, the monument to the 53rd Pennsylvania Infantry was dedicated on a rainy September morning in 1889. The unit was part of Caldwell's Division of the 2nd Corps. Driving the Confederates across the Wheatfield along with other regiments of Brooke's Brigade, the 53rd Pennsylvania advanced to this position, which they held until the Union line in the Wheatfield area began to crumble.

When the regimental survivors formed a Veteran's Association in 1880, one of the first projects undertaken was the erection of a monument on the field. They raised $1500 towards the project which was matched when Pennsylvania appropriated an additional $1500. The available money was still not enough to hire a name sculptor so company artists employed by contractor H. Oursler and Sons undertook the task of designing a suitable monument. The design ultimately chosen, "The Sentinel", consists of a bronze statue in the complete winter uniform of a Union soldier. He stands watch over the position where the 53rd fought July 2, 1863.

[1] *Pennsylvania at Gettysburg*, 1:337–338.

LOCATION: BROOKE AVENUE
DEDICATED: SEPTEMBER 11, 1889
COST: $2700
SCULPTOR: G. WAGNER
CONTRACTOR: GRANITE–H. OURSLER & SONS
                BRONZE–HENRY BONNARD
                BRONZE CO.
MATERIAL: BARRE GRANITE
SPECIFICATIONS: 1ST BASE–6'0"SQ × 1'8"H
                2ND BASE–4'3"SQ × 1'3"H
                DIE–3'3"SQ × 4'H
                CAP–4'0"SQ × 3'0"H
                STATUE–7'6"
                TOTAL HEIGHT–17'6"

DWM

27th Connecticut Infantry

During the fighting in the Wheatfield on the evening of July 2, General John R. Brooke's Brigade, consisting of the 53rd and 145th Pennsylvania, 64th New York, 2nd Delaware, and 27th Connecticut Infantries, was thrown into the fighting. As these regiments swept across the field they broke through the Confederate defenders, driving them across a marshy, wooded area and up onto the high ground beyond. Here, along what is known as Brooke Avenue today, one will find the regimental monuments to Brooke's Brigade. One unit in that brigade has the unique distinction of having five memorials marking the path of its advance through this area. No other unit present here at Gettysburg has as many monuments to honor so few men as the 27th Connecticut Infantry.

FWH

LOCATION: BROOKE AVENUE
STATE SPONSORED MONUMENT
DEDICATED: APRIL 17, 1889
COST: $1000

LS

LOCATION: WHEATFIELD
REGIMENTAL ASSOCIATION MONUMENT
DEDICATED: OCTOBER 22, 1885
COST: $950
DESIGNER/CONTRACTOR: ST. JOHNSBURY CO.
MATERIAL: ST. JOHNSBURY GRANITE
SPECIFICATIONS:

At the battle of Chancellorsville, Virginia two months before Gettysburg, a full eight companies of the 27th had been captured by the Confederates. Those that remained, totalling seventy-five officers and men, were consolidated into two companies under the command of Lt. Colonel Henry C. Merwin. These men are the seventy-five individuals that the monuments honor. In the charge across the Wheatfield that afternoon, Merwin was killed at the site where the largest monument now stands. The monument is a tall granite shaft, topped by a large bronze eagle perched on two artillery tubes. This was erected by the Survivor's Association in October of 1885. At the same time an advance position marker was placed on the ridge above the Wheatfield to indicate the farthest point in the advance in the charge of July 2. This can be found in the woods about twenty yards behind the right flank marker of the 53rd Pennsylvania.

Several years later, when the state of Connecticut appropriated one thousand dollars for each regiment to mark the field, the survivors choose to use the money to place a more substantial monument on Brooke Avenue, joining monuments placed by the other four regiments of the brigade. The most prominent feature on this, as on all monuments sponsored by the state of Connecticut, is the large, raised seal of the state with the motto "Qui Transtulit Sustinet"—"He who transplanted still sustains." Other features include the trefoil 2nd Corps symbol worked into the design in several places and the carved sabres and muskets on each end of the die.

Two small commemorative markers complete the 27th Connecticut's set. The first, along Wheatfield Road, is marked:

"In Memory of
Lt. Col.
Henry C. Merwin
27th C.V.
who fell mortally
wounded where
the monument of his
regiment stands"

This marker was probably erected to draw attention to the unit's main monument set, as it was, well off of the developing tour roads, out in the cultivated fields. The second marker, at the southern end of the field along DeTrobriand Avenue, marks the spot where Captain Jedediah Chapman, commander of one of the 27th companies, was killed during the charge. Both of these commemorative markers were placed in the early 1890's.

DWM

17th Maine Infantry

DWM

Along the stone wall that borders the southern end of the Wheatfield, the men of the 17th Maine Infantry took position on the afternoon of July 2, 1863. Here they fought a stubborn defensive battle that would cost over one hundred casualties. Typical of many units of both armies at Gettysburg, the hard, forced marches to get to this field wore out the shoes

of the men to such an extent that many of the 17th went into battle that day barefooted. To add further to the men's discomfort, most had received no rations for twenty-four hours.[1]

The monument to the 17th, the costliest Maine monument erected on the field, was placed on the spot the unit's colors were located during the fight. To symbolize the unit's affiliation inset in the sides of the shaft are diamond shaped blocks of red granite. The red was the standard color of the badges of 1st Division units while the badge of the 3rd Corps was the diamond. The most interesting feature on the monument is the statue chiselled from a block of white Hallowell granite. Representing an alert infantryman holding his rifle "at the ready", the soldier holds a position behind a carved stone wall such as the one the unit fought behind that still remains near the monument's base. To further lend realism to the sculpture, trampled wheat can be seen around the soldier and wall indicative of the 1863 crop that gave this field the name it bears in history. Following the erection of the monument the bronze tablet was added. It contains the history of the regiment here at Gettysburg and throughout the war, and was placed to relate to future generations the historic record of the 17th Maine Infantry.

[1] Vanderslice, *Gettysburg Then and Now*, p. 207.

LOCATION: DETROBRIAND AVENUE
DEDICATED: OCTOBER 10, 1888
DESIGNER/CONTRACTOR: HALLOWELL GRANITE
MATERIAL: HALLOWELL GRANITE
SPECIFICATIONS: 1ST BASE–8'SQ × 2'3"H
2ND BASE–6'SQ × 2'8"H
SHAFT–4'3"SQ TAPER TO 3'8"SQ
CAP–4'4"SQ × 4'6"H
TOTAL HEIGHT–20'5"

The 4th Michigan Infantry was another unit that became embroiled in the fierce, chaotic fighting in the Wheatfield that July evening. On the front of the die is a bas relief officially described as ". . . a spirited life sized representation of a color bearer in action."[1] In reality it depicts the unit's regimental commander, Colonel Harrison H. Jeffords, described during the monument's dedication ". . . as brave a man as ever a traitor killed." Jeffords was shot and bayoneted on the spot by Confederate soldiers attempting to capture the flag of the unit.[2]

Flags were the heart and soul of the regiment, the symbol of all that the men were fighting for. The cry of "rally round the flag" was not a hollow one to the soldiers of that time. Usually presented by the governor of the state, mayors of cities, prominent businessmen, or the women of the town, the ceremonies to present the unit's flags were often filled with patriotic pleas and fervent promises to return the flag safely home, unsoiled by the touch of enemy hands. Such were the circumstances surrounding the flag of the 4th Michigan. Colonel Jeffords, his officers, and his men had all pledged to defend with their lives the flags presented to the unit at the outset of the war.

As the Confederates poured into the Wheatfield, the 4th Michigan became involved in a close hand-to-hand fight. At one point several Confederate soldiers managed to grab the 4th's flag from its colorbearer. Jeffords, with drawn sword, rushed in slashing at the man holding his flag. Striking down the Confederate Jeffords grabbed the flag and began to withdraw. Unwilling to let that valued trophy of battle escape, several Confederates bayoneted the Colonel and regained the flag. Before they could get away with the prize some soldiers of the 4th rushed in and in a short, desperate struggle, succeeded in recapturing the flag. They carried it to safety along with the body of their fallen commander.[3]

When designs for the monument were solicited from the veterans, the concensus was that the most appropriate person to honor on this memorial was their fallen Colonel. Today he stands holding a representation of the flag he died defending.

[1] Michigan Monument Commission, *Michigan at Gettysburg, July 1st, 2nd, and 3rd, 1863. June 12th, 1889,* (Detroit: Winn and Hammond, Printers and Binders, 1889), p. 81.

[2] Ibid., pp. 64, 81; See also Vanderslice, *Gettysburg Then and Now,* p. 463.

[3] *Michigan at Gettysburg*, p. 86.

DWM

LOCATION: SICKLES AVENUE
DEDICATED: JUNE 12, 1889
COST: $1350
CONTRACTOR: GRANITE–MITCHELL GRANITE
        CO.
        BRONZE–AMERICAN BRONZE CO.
MATERIAL: OAK HILL GRANITE STANDARD
        BRONZE
SPECIFICATIONS: 7′L × 5′2″W × 13.5′H

Irish Brigade Monument

On the high ground west of the Wheatfield there is a large concentration of monuments to Union regiments from several brigades that had fought their way through the Wheatfield. One quite distinctive monument in this area is that of the Irish Brigade, a unit organized by former Irish revolutionary Thomas Francis Meagher. Active in most of the major eastern battles of the Civil War, the brigade was shattered at Fredericksburg and Chancellorsville. Fighting under the emerald green regimental flags decorated with the harp of Erin were five all-Irish regiments, the 63rd, 69th, and 88th New York, 28th Massachusetts, and 116th Pennsylvania Infantries. At Gettysburg the entire brigade numbered just five hundred and thirty men, the size of a severely understrength regiment. The battle here on July 2 would cost the unit two hundred and fourteen casualties.

The Irish Brigade monument honors the three New York regiments of the brigade who combined their state appropriations for this purpose. The shaft of polished granite and inset bronze is carved in the shape of a traditional symbol of Ireland, the Celtic cross. At the top of the cross is the trefoil symbol of the 2nd Army Corps. Beneath it are five medallions with the numeric designation of the three regiments, the state seal of New York, and the seal of Ireland. At the base lies a life size Irish wolf hound in bronze, representing faith and devotion.[1]

An additional feature of the memorial is the bronze plaque on the right face of the base representing a section of an artillery battery in action. This was meant to honor Captain James Rorty's 14th New York Independent Battery. This unit had been mustered in to United States service as part of the original Irish Brigade in 1861. Detached later in the war, the battery participated in the battle of Gettysburg on July 3, suffering several casualties. The veterans of the Irish Brigade chose to include their former artillery comrades on their memorial.

[1] *New York at Gettysburg*, 2:482.

LOCATION: SICKLES AVENUE, THE LOOP
DEDICATED: JULY 2, 1888
COST: $5000
SCULPTOR: WILLIAM RUDOLPH O'DONOVAN
DESIGNER: JOHN H. DUNCAN
CONTRACTOR: MAURICE J. POWERS
MATERIAL: GETTYSBURG GRANITE
        QUINCY GRANITE
        STANDARD BRONZE
SPECIFICATIONS: BASE–10'2"L × 8'W × 19'6"H
        BRONZE CROSS–1'8"W × 11'4"H
        FRONT TABLET–7'5"L × 1'0"W
        REAR TABLET–4'1"L × 1'0"W

LS

66th New York Infantry

In an army of unique units tied to particular geographic areas or identified with a preponderance of one ethnic group, the 66th New York Infantry did not stand out. Lost among the "Brooklyn Chasseurs", the "Irish Brigades", the "German Regiments", the brigades of "Iron", and the colorful Zouaves, one former member described the 66th as an "... ordinary, every-day regiment."[1] Its members came from all over the state of New York and included many from Maine and Massachusetts. Many Irish and German immigrants enlisted, but not in sufficient numbers to give the unit an ethnic identity.

One of many units to charge across the increasingly bloody Wheatfield that afternoon, the 66th lost forty-four casualties during the action. Their monument is placed at the most advanced point reached during the charge. Like the unit itself, the monument does not stand out and has no unique design to draw people's attention. Aside from the corps symbol, little ornamentation exists on the die.

Perhaps the most noteworthy feature, hardly ever seen, is the bronze plaque on the back entitled "Peace and Unity". It portrays two soldiers, one Union, one Confederate, in the act of shaking hands.

[1] *New York at Gettysburg*, 2:552–555.

LS

LOCATION: SICKLES AVENUE AT THE LOOP
DEDICATED: OCTOBER 9, 1889
COST: $1500
SCULPTOR: BYRON M. PICKETT
DESIGNER/CONTRACTOR: MAURICE J. POWERS
MATERIAL: HALLOWELL, ME. GRANITE
        STANDARD BRONZE
SPECIFICATIONS: 7'0"L × 6'3"W × 13'9"H
        BRONZE ALTO RELIEVO 2'0" ×
        4'0"

LS

32nd Massachusetts Infantry

The monument to the 32nd Massachusetts Infantry was carved to resemble a soldier's shelter tent, more commonly called a "pup tent." It was designed by S. C. Spaulding, a veteran who had served in the unit during the war. The "pup tent" was such an everpresent feature of the soldier's everyday life that the theme of the monument is quite appropriate.

It is located today where the firing line of the 32nd Massachusetts was located as they participated in the Wheatfield defense and fighting. Many of the casualties sustained by the unit here were carried about fifty yards to the rear. There, an advanced field hospital was established by one of the unit's surgeons, Z. Boylston Adams. At this site, Adams patched up and stabilized the wounded as thoroughly as possible before sending them to a larger field hospital in the rear. A year after the dedication of the pup tent monument in 1894, the Veteran's Association placed a bronze plaque on the group of boulders that sheltered the wounded that day. This pile of boulders is directly behind the monument of the 5th Michigan Infantry.

LOCATION: SICKLES AVENUE AT THE LOOP
DEDICATED: OCTOBER 1894
COST: $500
DESIGNER: S. C. SPAULDING

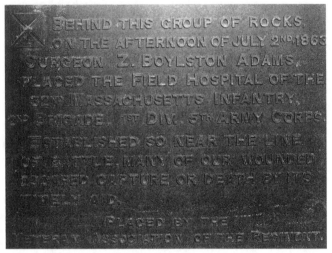

LS

FWH

2nd Andrews Sharpshooters (Massachusetts)

Another unit that fought in the Wheatfield/Loop area was a small detachment of Massachusetts sharpshooters, a specialized unit made up of men chosen for exceptional marksmanship. Known as the 2nd Andrew Sharpshooters, they were named for the war-governor of the state, John A. Andrews, and were armed with very heavy rifles equipped with crude telescopes.[1] These were similar to one on display in the park's Visitor Center. The Sharpshooters' Veteran's Association created a different type of memorial than usually found on the field.

The monument consists of a carved granite soldier in complete uniform standing as if taking cover behind a large boulder. Not resting on a traditional base, the soldier presents a somewhat startling and lifelike appearance as one passes by. Cut from a single block of granite, the sculptor did not have sufficient material available to completely carve the rifle giving the monument a somewhat unfinished look. As with all Massachusetts monuments, detailed inscriptions are lacking.

[1] C. A. Stevens, *Berdan's United States Sharpshooters in the Army of the Potomac,* (Dayton, Ohio: Press of Morningside Bookshop, 1984), p. 205.

LOCATION: SICKLES AVENUE AT THE LOOP
DEDICATED: OCTOBER 8, 1885
COST: $500
DESIGNER/CONTRACTOR: BOSTON MARBLE &
                GRANITE CO

FWH

28th Massachusetts Infantry

The last and the largest of the units of the Irish Brigade at Gettysburg was the 28th Massachusetts Infantry. Two hundred twenty soldiers fought along the line marked by the regimental monument today. Perched atop the monument, the most prominent feature is the large granite eagle with folded wings, symbolizing peace. The unit's Irish identity is evident with the Irish harp carved on the left face of the monument. The Gaelic slogan underneath the seal of the United States, "Faugh A Ballaugh", is roughly translated "Clear the Way". Apparently, this slogan was the rallying cry, not only of the 28th, but other Irish units at Gettysburg.

LOCATION: SICKLES AVENUE AT THE LOOP
DEDICATED: JULY 2, 1886
COST: $500
DESIGNER/CONTRACTOR: P. M. BRADFORD

FWH

116th Pennsylvania Infantry

The 116th Pennsylvania Infantry was another member of the Irish Brigade. Like the three New York regiments of the unit, the 116th had suffered heavy casualties in prior battles and these losses had not been replaced. Civil War regiments at full strength normally consisted of ten companies of one hundred men each, totalling one thousand soldiers. At Gettysburg, one hundred and forty-two officers and men remained to march into battle under the flag of the 116th. By the evening of July 2, casualties had reduced the unit to the size of a normal company.

The monument erected by the survivors of the regiment deals with a different theme than most others on the field. Bravery, courage, loyalty, devotion, and steadfastness in battle are common traits of the monuments on this and other fields. Few deal with the brutal realities of warfare's destructiveness as effectively as the 116th Pennsylvania. During the battle the regiment was under the command of Major St. Clair A. Mulholland. Upon arriving at this position a lull occurred in the fighting. The Major walked a short distance forward to where the 110th Pennsylvania had fought earlier in the afternoon. He was awed by the sight of one of the dead in partic-

ular, a young soldier, shot through the head. A faint smile was visible on the dead boy's quiet, upturned face.[1] Mulholland never forgot that haunting scene. Years later it inspired the design of the present monument. The sculpture represents a small portion of battlefield that the fighting has passed by. A dead soldier, similar to the one Mulholland described, lies quietly beside the wall where he and his comrades had earlier fought. The closeness of the combat is suggested by the position of the musket, still gripped by the muzzle. As he received the fatal wound, he was using the musket as a club to defend his position. The broken bayonet scabbard, splintered musket, and the remains of a farmer's fence underscore the destruction left in the path of the fighting. No hint is given as to the outcome of the struggle here. Death is the only victor reflected in the monument. For the handful of survivors of the 116th Pennsylvania Infantry, reflecting back on the comrades left behind on many fields of that war, death had reaped a tremendous harvest from their ranks.

[1] St. Clair A. Mulholland, *The Story of the 116th Regiment, Pennsylvania Infantry,* (Philadelphia: F. McManus, Jr. and Company, 1899), p. 138.

LOCATION: SICKLES AVENUE AT THE LOOP
DEDICATED: SEPTEMBER 11, 1889
COST: $3165
SCULPTOR: J. H. KELLY
DESIGNER/CONTRACTOR: HEINS AND BYE
MATERIAL: BASE–QUINCY GRANITE
         STATUE–CONCORD GRANITE

SPECIFICATIONS: 1ST BS–9'6"L × 5'8"W × 1'10"H
         2ND BS–8'L × 4'2"W × 3'H
         CAP/DIE–7'L × 4'2"W × 4'6"H
         TOTAL HEIGHT–9'4"
         WEIGHT–34 TONS

REF

9th Massachusetts Battery

As General Daniel Sickles' 3rd Army Corps attempted to hold out against the pressure exerted in the attack of Longstreet's Corps of the Confederate Army, reinforcements were sent in to bolster the thin Union line. One of these reinforcing units was the 9th Massachusetts Battery of six 12-pounder Napoleon guns. Firing initially from the position indicated by the monument today, the 9th Battery did tremendous damage to the Confederate regiments crossing the Rose Farm. The Confederate breakthrough in the Wheatfield and the Peach Orchard jeopardized the battery's position and necessitated a withdrawal to the Trostle farm. Unable to limber up the guns due to the sharpshooter's fire from the area of the Wheatfield, the guns were attached to long ropes called prolonges to allow them to continue firing as the horses pulled them to the rear. The guns fired canister rounds to keep the Confederate infantry in front at a distance. The right sections used solid shot fired towards the Peach Orchard to slow the advance from that sector. Eventually the unit arrived at the Trostle farm where orders were received to hold this new position at all costs to buy time to establish a new line in the rear. Here the 9th made a final stand, firing until the guns were overrun and most of the men struck down. The battery commander, Captain John Bigelow, was wounded near the second position. His bugler, Charles Reed, rode up to him, dismounted, and helped Bigelow onto his horse. He then took the reins in hand and under a heavy Confederate fire, calmly led Bigelow to safety. For this heroic act, Reed was awarded a Medal of Honor.

The defensive stand of the 9th Massachusetts that day cost the battery three of its four officers, six out of seven sergeants, and twenty-eight of the sixty enlisted men. Out of the eighty-eight horses assigned to the battery, sixty were killed in the fight and twenty more disabled. In delaying the Confederate assault, the battery fired over three tons of ammunition from its six guns, including thirty-two rounds of canister. At the close of the action, only four canister rounds remained in the limber chests.[1]

The 9th Massachusetts is represented on the field today by three monuments marking each position the battery held on the field. These positions

DWM

LOCATION: WHEATFIELD ROAD
DEDICATED: OCTOBER 19, 1885
COST: $1000
DESIGNERS: JOHN BIGELOW
　　　　　　CHARLES REED
CONTRACTOR: BOSTON MARBLE & GRANITE CO
MATERIAL: QUINCY GRANITE
SPECIFICATIONS: 4'L × 3'W × 9'H

had been identified by the monument committee of the Veteran's Association in the fall of 1883. The locations of the monuments of the 9th Massachusetts were determined the way many other memorial sites were chosen. Representatives of the veterans usually met with the Memorial Association's official, John Bachelder, and walked the field until a concensus could be reached on the exact location their unit had occupied. In the case of the 9th, a number of veterans, including Bigelow, walked to the Trostle farm where the battery had made its last stand that day. From there each man separately went across the field to locate the first position. All concurred with the location.[2]

The designs for the monuments, suggested by Bigelow, were laid out by a well known Boston artist, C. W. Reed, the same man who twenty-one years before rode back to rescue the wounded Bigelow. The main monument is placed on the spot where the left gun was in position. On its front is a laurel wreath symbolic of victory, and a palm frond, symbolizing peace. Thirty-nine carved cannonballs form the border for the inscription.[3] Four hundred yards away at the Trostle farm, is a block of granite carved in the shape of an ammunition chest. This marks the scene of the battery's final stand on July 2. In Zeigler's grove, near the Cyclorama Center, a small stone with a carved artillery haversack locates the position of the battery's remnant on July 3 and 4: two guns and the surviving men under the command of the sole unwounded officer.

[1] Major John Bigelow, *The Peach Orchard: Gettysburg July 2, 1863,* (Minneapolis: Kimball-Storer Co., 1910; reprint ed., Butternut and Blue, 1984), p. 61.

[2] Levi W. Baker, *History of the Ninth Massachusetts Battery,* (South Framingham: Lakeview Press, 1888), p. 209.

[3] Ibid., p. 21.

Hampton's Battery F Independent Pennsylvania Light Artillery

Due to the tremendous casualties suffered in prior battles, the remnant of Captain Robert Hampton's Battery F, Pennsylvania Artillery, fought as part of another battery in the defense of the Peach Orchard the afternoon of July 2. Atop the granite base of the monument is a fine bronze statue of a cannoneer with a rammer. The upper end of the rammer was used to sponge out the tube after each discharge to extinguish any lingering sparks prior to inserting the next charge. The cup on the opposite end of the rammer staff was used to push the shell down the tube. This artilleryman stands as if watching the flight of the shell just fired.

The most prominent feature on the front of the granite base is a large bronze casting of a large eagle. This eagle is supported by the Great Seal of the United States and the seal of the Commonwealth of Pennsylvania. Intertwined with the casting is the traditional symbol of victory, the wreath of laurel.

FWH

LOCATION: WHEATFIELD ROAD AT THE PEACH ORCHARD
DEDICATED: NOVEMBER 1890
COST: $1940
SCULPTOR: C. F. HAMILTON
CONTRACTOR: ALFRED E. WINDOR AND COMPANY
MATERIAL: WESTERLY GRANITE STANDARD BRONZE
SPECIFICATIONS: STATUE–6′HIGH

7th New Jersey Infantry

The monument to the 7th New Jersey Infantry was erected on the spot where its commander Colonel Louis R. Francine was killed during the height of the battle on the evening of July 2. Consisting of two blocks of Quincy granite, it is carved in the shape of a correctly proportioned minie bullet. It stands alone in the field where the unit supported Graham's brigade in its fight to defend the Peach Orchard heights. The minie bullet was the most common type of ammunition used in the battle of Gettysburg. Named after its developer, French army Captain Claude-Etienne Minie, the design of the projectile enabled speedy loading and accurate firing. These two features were sadly lacking with the old musket ball. The minie bullet was small enough to easily slip down even a powder clogged barrel. A small cavity in the base caught the gasses created by the powder charge's explosion. These gasses then caused the soft lead to expand to tightly fill the barrel and grip the rifling grooves, increasing the speed of the projectile and its accuracy.[1] Minie bullets were of such significance to the soldiers of both armies that you will find carvings of them on many battlefield monuments. The veterans of the 7th New Jersey chose it as the most dominant feature of their memorial.

[1] Faust, *Encyclopedia of the Civil War,* pp. 497–498.

LOCATION: SICKLES AVENUE
              ACROSS FROM EXCELSIOR FIELD
DEDICATED: JUNE 30, 1888
COST: $1175
DESIGNER/CONTRACTOR: FREDERICK AND FIELD
MATERIAL: LIGHT QUINCY GRANITE
              DARK QUINCY GRANITE
SPECIFICATIONS: 1ST BASE–6′ SQ
              BULLET–3′2″ DIA
              HEIGHT–10′6″
              WEIGHT–12 TONS

FWH

Excelsior Brigade Monument

At the outbreak of the Civil War, former Democratic Congressman Daniel E. Sickles undertook the task of raising an entire brigade for service in putting down the rebellion. The five regiments raised, the 70th, 71st, 72nd, 73rd, and 74th New York Infantries, fought as reinforcements to beleaguered units all along the Union lines on the Emmitsburg Road. Therefore the monument to the five regiments of the Excelsior brigade is located on a site representative of a central position. Each regimental veteran's association had the option to erect individual monuments but as the five regiments had always been united in service and comradeship, they decided to unite and build a single, large brigade monument.[1]

The cornerstone of this memorial was laid on the twenty-fifth anniversary of the battle: July 2, 1888.[2] The completed monument consists of a pentagonal base with each of the five sides devoted to a plaque detailing the history of one of the Excelsior's regiments. The five highly polished columns surrounding the empty pedestal are also representative of the five regiments. It was originally intended that a bust of General Sickles, commander of the Union 3rd Corps in the battle, be placed on the inner pedestal, but this was never completed. At the top of the dome a large, bronze eagle sits in a warlike, outstretched wing-pose symbolic of the old Excelsior brigade's readiness to strike out against their country's enemies.

[1] *New York at Gettysburg,* 2:585.
[2] Ibid., 2:574.

LS

LOCATION: SICKLES AVENUE AT EXCELSIOR
        FIELD
DEDICATED: JULY 2, 1893
COST: $7500
SCULPTOR: THEODORE BAUER
CONTRACTOR: GRANITE–NORTH EAST
        MONUMENT CO.
        BRONZE–MAURICE J. POWER
MATERIAL: CONCORD, N.H. GRANITE
        KEESEVILLE, N.Y. HYPERSTHENE
        GRANITE
        STANDARD BRONZE
SPECIFICATIONS: PENTAGONAL–6'2" EA. SIDE
        HEIGHT–21'7"
        SIDE TABLETS–4'3"L × 1'10"H
        FRIEZE TABLETS–5'6"L × 1'6"H
        EAGLE–2'9"H

73rd New York Infantry (2nd Fire Zouaves)

Nearly ten years after the erection of the Excelsior Brigade Monument, the former volunteer firemen of New York City erected a regimental monument to honor one of the units of the brigade, the 73rd New York Infantry, commonly known as the 2nd Fire Zouaves. In May of 1861, Chief Engineer John Decker called a meeting of all members of the city's volunteer fire department for the purpose of raising a regiment. Many of the city's firemen enlisted in the unit. Throughout the duration of their service, each of these soldier's names was kept on the rolls as active firefighters in New York.[1]

The monument was designed to commemorate the unit's service throughout the Civil War, not just here on this battlefield.[2] Placed where they fought on July 2, the monument consists of a bronze statue of two men, one in the uniform of a Union infantryman, the second dressed as a New York volunteer fireman. Each holds a tool of his trade in hand, the soldier's musket, and the fireman's calling horn. The monument's design was quite appropriate to portray the dual identity of many of the men of the 73rd.

[1] *New York at Gettysburg*, 2:600.
[2] Ibid., p. 603.

LOCATION: EXCELSIOR FIELD
DEDICATED: SEPTEMBER 6, 1897
COST: $5000
SCULPTOR: JOSEPH MORETTI
DESIGNER/CONTRACTOR: HOFFMAN AND
                              PROCHAZKA
MATERIAL: BARRE, VT. GRANITE
              STANDARD BRONZE
SPECIFICATIONS: BASE–8′L × 7′W × 14′H
                 STATUE–4′L × 3′W × 7′H
                 FRONT/REAR TABLETS–3′L ×
                 2′H
                 SIDE TABLETS–2′ SQ

LS

New Jersey Brigade

Atop a wooded knoll overlooking the George Weikert farm, the forty foot "watchtower" of the 1st New Jersey brigade was erected twenty-five years after the battle of Gettysburg. During the fighting on this end of the field, the brigade, consisting of the 1st, 2nd, 3rd, 4th, and 15th New Jersey Infantry regiments, remained in reserve, ready to participate in defending the line wherever needed.

The brigade's Veteran's Association purchased the entire Weikert farm to preserve the positions the units held during the battle.[1] Rather than erect individual regimental monuments to each one, the large tower design was chosen to commemorate the services of all. The site selected was a point located in the rear of the center of the brigade's battle line. The illusion of a tower is heightened by the columns on each side which hint at an entranceway. Window-like embrasures on the side and around the top enhances this image. Each course of the tower consists of a single stone seven feet in diameter.[2] On either side of the shaft are bronze medallions honoring two of the unit's commanders: General Philip Kearny, the original organizer of the brigade, and General Alfred T. A. Torbert, its commander during the battle. The contract for erecting the watchtower also included small, individual markers to note the approximate position of each unit on July 3. These can be found at the base of the little knoll on which the brigade monument stands today.

FWH

[1] New Jersey Battlefield Monuments Commission, *Final Report of the Gettysburg Battlefield Commission of New Jersey, dated October 1, 1891,* (Trenton, N.J.: The John L. Murphy Publishing Co., 1891), p. 21; Samuel Toombs, *New Jersey Troops in the Gettysburg Campaign from June 5 to July 31, 1863,* (Orange, N.J.: The Evening Mail Publishing House, 1888), pp. 344–345.

[2] New Jersey Battlefield Monuments Commission, *Report of the Commission to Care For Gettysburg Battle Monuments, 1892,* (Trenton, N.J.: Naar, Day, and Naas, Printers, 1893), p. 17.

LOCATION: SEDGWICK AVENUE
DEDICATED: JUNE 30, 1888
COST: $5700
DESIGNER/CONTRACTOR: NEW ENGLAND
                       MONUMENT CO.
                       BUREAU BROTHERS
MATERIAL: GETTYSBURG GRANITE
             QUINCY GRANITE
             HALLOWELL GRANITE
             STANDARD BRONZE
SPECIFICATIONS: DIAMETER 7'
                     HEIGHT 40'

Father William Corby Portrait Statue

The portrait statue of Father William Corby honors one of the hundreds of chaplains present with the armies at Gettysburg. Serving in the capacity of chaplain of the Irish brigade's 88th New York Infantry, Corby's actions the afternoon of July 2 were to be remembered as part of the rich folk lore of this battle. As the pressure on General Sickle's 3rd Corps increased, reinforcements were rushed in to bolster the line. General Winfield Scott Hancock ordered one of his divisional commanders, General John C. Caldwell, to move his unit to the relief of the embattled regiments of Sickle's corps. Among Caldwell's four brigades was Patrick Kelly's Irish brigade. While the regiments began to form up, Father Corby went to the front of the column and asked permission to delay the movement a few minutes while he spoke to the men. Stepping atop a boulder, he raised his right hand and as the men stood with bowed heads, the sound of battle raging to the south and west, Corby called upon God to grant them courage, then pronounced general absolution. The brigade marched off into battle.[1] Following the Civil War, Corby's service to his fellow men included two terms as president of the University of Notre Dame.

Nearly a half century after Corby's actions at Gettysburg, General St. Clair A. Mulholland, an eyewitness to the event, enlisted the aid of the four hundred member Catholic Alumni Society to honor the chaplain with a portrait statue on the field.[2] Using funds raised within the Catholic community, this statue was created of Father Corby posed at the moment of pronouncing absolution. It was mounted on the site where the event actually took place and in some accounts, on the exact boulder.[3] An identical copy of the statue was placed on the campus of Notre Dame the following year.

[1] *Pennsylvania at Gettysburg,* 2:627–628; Grimm and Roy, *Human Interest Stories,* p. 10.
[2] Craven, *Sculptures at Gettysburg,* pp. 71, 73.
[3] Ibid., p. 71; Gettysburg Compiler, October 16, 1910.

LOCATION: SOUTH HANCOCK AVENUE
DEDICATED: OCTOBER 29, 1910
SCULPTOR: SAMUEL MURRAY
CONTRACTOR: ROMAN BRONZE WORKS
MATERIAL: STANDARD BRONZE

LS

New York Auxiliary Monument

One of the more recent Union memorials on the field at Gettysburg is the New York Auxiliary monument. New York had nineteen native-sons serving as general officers in command of corps, divisions, or brigades at Gettysburg, yet statues had been created to honor only eight.[1] The New York Battlefield Monuments Commission decided to complete the historic record by creating a single memorial to honor all New Yorkers, from the rank of major to major-general who commanded units at Gettysburg. Thirty-nine men were to be included, to which were added the names of the army's provost marshal, Marsena Patrick, and the chief of staff, General Daniel Butterfield, both native New Yorkers.

The monument consists of a large exedra of Concord granite.[2] Heavy marble tiles form the patio,

the design of which radiates outward from the center. Prominent in the middle of the wall is a large granite eagle and laurel victor's wreath. The names and commands of each of the forty-one honored officers are carved on the panels. At the dedication ceremonies in 1925, nearly one hundred aging Civil War veterans were in attendance. Two-thirds of them had participated in the battle over sixty years before.

[1] These were Doubleday, Wadsworth, Robinson, Barlow, Hays, Warren, Green, and Slocum.

[2] An exedra is a classical style of architecture which consists of a circular wall containing a curved bench. In the days of the Greeks and Romans this is where discussions were held.

FWH

LOCATION: SOUTH HANCOCK AVENUE
DEDICATED: SEPTEMBER 9, 1925
COST: $27,875
SCULPTOR: GEROME BRUSH
ARCHITECT: EDWARD PEARCE CASEY
CONTRACTOR: JOHN SWENSON GRANITE CO.
MATERIAL: CONCORD GRANITE
SPECIFICATIONS: WIDTH—42'
                DEPTH—24'
                HEIGHT (AT EAGLE) 21'
                TOTAL PANELS—18

1st Minnesota Infantry

At the onset of the Civil War, the governor of Minnesota declared "... we are a young state, not very numerous or powerful, but we are for the Union as it is, and the Constitution as it is."[1] With those words the new state prepared to contribute what men and material it could to support the Union war effort. In the Army of the Potomac, one regiment, the 1st Minnesota Infantry, provided the state's contribution in the east. Consisting of three hundred and thirty men at Gettysburg, its actions during the battle would provide a lasting reputation in the annals of warfare. On the evening of July 2 as the decimated remnants of the 3rd Corps finally were overwhelmed, the victorious Confederates were poised to seal their victory by continuing on and capturing the now sparsely defended Cemetery Ridge. Officers began to quickly piece together a line of artillery batteries to defend the position and provide a haven for the defeated Union regiments to rally behind. General Hancock, the Union 2nd Corps commander, looked for available units to buy the Union the valuable time it needed to complete the line by holding the Confederates at bay. The men of the 1st Minnesota were available. Eight companies of the regiment were ordered to charge and two hundred sixty-two men moved down into the low ground in front of the present monument. There they engaged the enemy. At a staggering loss of two hundred fifteen casualties they managed to blunt the Confederate advance sufficiently to allow other units to reach the area to complete the repulse. The total loss to the unit was 82% in this single action, a percentage not equalled by any other unit prior to the Civil War. Hancock said of the charge "There is no more gallant deed recorded in history."[2] The next afternoon the handful of survivors were once again called upon to throw themselves into battle to aide in repulsing Pickett's charge, an action in which seventeen more Minnesotans fell.

In 1867 the survivors of the 1st Minnesota placed a marble memorial urn among the graves of fifty-two of their fallen comrades in the National Cemetery. Twenty-six years later, the state of Minnesota erected the large state monument on the site where the charge of July 2 began.[3] A secondary marker south of the clump of trees denotes the unit's position of July 3. A bronze plaque on the base of the main monument depicts the impetuous charge that contributed so greatly in turning back the Confederate tide at Gettysburg on July 2. Atop the base, a bronze soldier portrayed at a "double quick" pace, faces the ravine where the 1st Minnesota lost so heavily.

[1] Faust, *Encyclopedia of the Civil War*, p. 498.
[2] Ibid.
[3] Vanderslice, *Gettysburg Then and Now*, p. 467; Gettysburg National Military Park Commission, *Annual Reports of the Gettysburg National Military Park Commission to the Secretary of War, 1893–1904*, (Washington: Government Printing Office, 1905), Report of 1897, p. 39.

LOCATION: SOUTH HANCOCK AVENUE
BUILT: 1893
DEDICATED: JULY 2, 1897
COST: $16,000
SCULPTOR: JACOB H. FJELDE
CONTRACTOR: HENRY BONNARD BRONZE
COMPANY
MATERIAL: STANDARD BRONZE

LS

Pennsylvania State Memorial

Perhaps the most photographed monument on the battlefield today is the massive, domed Pennsylvania State Memorial. As the Fiftieth Anniversary of the battle of Gettysburg approached, a movement was begun to erect a single memorial to honor all Pennsylvanians who participated in the greatest battle ever to have been fought on the state's soil. In 1907, $150,000 was appropriated to design and erect a suitable memorial and a contest was held to solicit appropriate designs. Fifty-one designs and thirty plaster models were submitted to the committee for judging. One developed by architect W. Liance Cottrell of New York was selected and the Harrison Granite Company was chosen to execute the design.[1] Construction was begun in the early summer of 1909.

An incredible amount of material went into the building of the memorial; 1252 tons of cut granite, 1410 tons of broken stone, 740 tons of sand, 366 tons of cement, 50 tons of steel bars, and 22 tons of bronze.[2] Harrison was also responsible for creating ninety bronze tablets to contain the names of every Pennsylvanian who fought at Gettysburg. The work of casting these was subcontracted to the Federal Brass and Bronze Company of Astoria New York. They were given the task of creating the ninety tablets in slightly under six months. At one point the company turned out twenty-one tablets in twenty-one working days. The last one was completed and set into place on the parapet just hours before the dedication ceremonies began.[3]

The names on the tablets created unforeseen problems. Originally 34,530 names were inscribed with each tablet containing the names of the members of one regiment, organized according to company. These rosters were taken from the original army payroll forms of June 30, 1863, on file in the offices of the U.S. Treasury Department. They frequently contained misspellings, names of men dead but not yet removed from the rolls, men missing or captured in previous battles, men listed as deserters, and the names of many serving on detached duty, therefore not present a the time the battle was fought.[4] Shortly after the dedication additional funds were appropriated to correct, insert, and remove names; this work continues today.

The memorial consists of a massive dome supported by four archways, each flanked by Ionic columns. Atop the dome is a twenty-one foot high statue of the "Goddess of Victory and Peace" sculpted by Samuel Murray of Philadelphia. Weighing 7,500 pounds, it was cast from bronze taken from melting down cannon actually used in the war.[5] In the statue's right hand a sword is held aloft while her left holds the palm leaf of peace. "Victory's" purpose was to ". . . [signal] from this onetime battlefield, Pennsylvania's message to the world that war should cease and that peace reign amongst the nations of the earth."[6]

Above each archway are granite monoliths containing battle scenes honoring the four branches of service. Also sculpted by Murray, each one is nine feet high by eighteen feet long and consists of a solid block of granite weighing twenty-five tons. The scene honoring Pennsylvania's infantrymen depicts the fight of the "Bucktail Brigade" around the McPherson barn on the morning of July 1. The cavalry is accurately depicted on the south monolith, Murray having used a photograph of horses in action to faithfully sculpt the scene. The signal corps is honored on the east face while Pennsylvania's artillerymen are commemorated on the north monolith.

Murray was also responsible for carving the classical maidens in the spandrels above and flanking the arches. These serve as the attendants to "Victory" and each holds a trumpet or a victor's wreath.[7] Carved on the pediment beneath the dome are the names of thirty-four general officers from Pennsylvania who commanded troops during the battle.

At the time of the dedication, the eight portrait statues Cottrell envisioned as filling the niches on either side of each arch were missing due to the lack of funds. This was rectified the year following the dedication when an additional $40,000 was appropriated to create these statues. Van Amringe Granite Company of Boston, Massachusetts was given the contract. As it was desired to have the statues in place in time for the upcoming Fiftieth Anniversary celebration, the company had less than two years to complete the work. These portrait statues, each of which is eight feet high, represent President Abraham Lincoln, the only non-Pennsylvanian honored on the monument, the state's war-governor, Andrew Curtin, army commander George G. Meade, 1st Corps commander John Reynolds, and 2nd Corps commander Winfield Scott Hancock. Major-General David Birney, who commanded the 3rd Corps after Sickle's wounding and Alfred Pleasonton the army's cavalry commander also have statues. The eighth statue honors David Gregg, a commander of a cavalry division. Sculptor J. Otto Schweizer was responsible for "Lincoln", "Pleasonton", and "Gregg" while Lee Lawrie crafted "Meade", "Reynolds", and "Birney". The statue of "Andrew Curtin" was the work of W. Clark Noble and Cyrus Dallin created "Hancock".

Each statue was cast at the Gorham Manufacturing Company of Providence, Rhode Island and all were completed and set in place in the spring of 1913, two months ahead of schedule.[8] At a cost of nearly $200,000, the Pennsylvania Memorial is by far the most expensive of the battlefield monuments.

[1] *Pennsylvania at Gettysburg*, 2:37. Cottrell was the winner of the $500 1st prize. Richard C. Loss of Philadelphia was awarded the $350 second prize while the $150 3rd prize went to W. G. Sloan and J. H. Pershing.

[2] Ibid., p. 59.

[3] Ibid., p. 38.

[4] Ibid., p. 39.

[5] Ibid., p. 555.

[6] Ibid., p. 44.

[7] Ibid., p. 37; Craven, *Sculptures at Gettysburg*, p. 28.

[8] Ibid., pp. 60–61.

LS

LOCATION: HANCOCK AVENUE
DEDICATED: SEPTEMBER 27, 1910
COST: $182,000
ARCHITECT: W. LIANCE COTTRELL
SCULPTOR: SAMUEL MURRAY
CONTRACTOR: HARRISON GRANITE COMPANY
MATERIAL: MT. AIRY, N.C. GRANITE
SPECIFICATIONS: PARAPET–84'SQ
                MAIN MEMORIAL–40'SQ
                HEIGHT–69'

15th and 50th New York Engineers

Engineers performed a variety of duties for both armies. They helped design defenses, undertook topographical surveys, drew maps, and built roads and bridges. Two engineer regiments serving with the Army of the Potomac have a memorial on the field. The 15th and 50th New York Engineers combined their state monument appropriation to erect a joint engineer memorial.[1]

The monument's design is a turreted castle, the traditional symbol of the Corps of Engineers. In ad-

dition to brief histories of the two regiments, and the replicas of an Engineer officer's button, the main feature is a large bronze plaque near the top of the center tower. This depicts a set of pontoon bridges spanning a river. Engineer-constructed pontoon bridges aided the armies of both North and South to efficiently and safely cross rivers throughout the Gettysburg campaign.

[1] *New York at Gettysburg*, 3:1086.

KLS

LOCATION: PLEASONTON AVENUE
DEDICATED: SEPTEMBER 17, 1890
COST: $3,000
CONTRACTOR: FREDERICK AND FIELD
MATERIAL: QUINCY GRANITE
SPECIFICATIONS: BASE—14'3"L × 4'9"W
    HEIGHT—12'0"
    PONTOON RELIEF—2'L × 1'4"H
    OFFICERS BUTTONS—8" DIA
    TABLETS—2'L × 1'5"H

SECTION FOUR: THE SECOND DAY'S BATTLEFIELD NORTH END

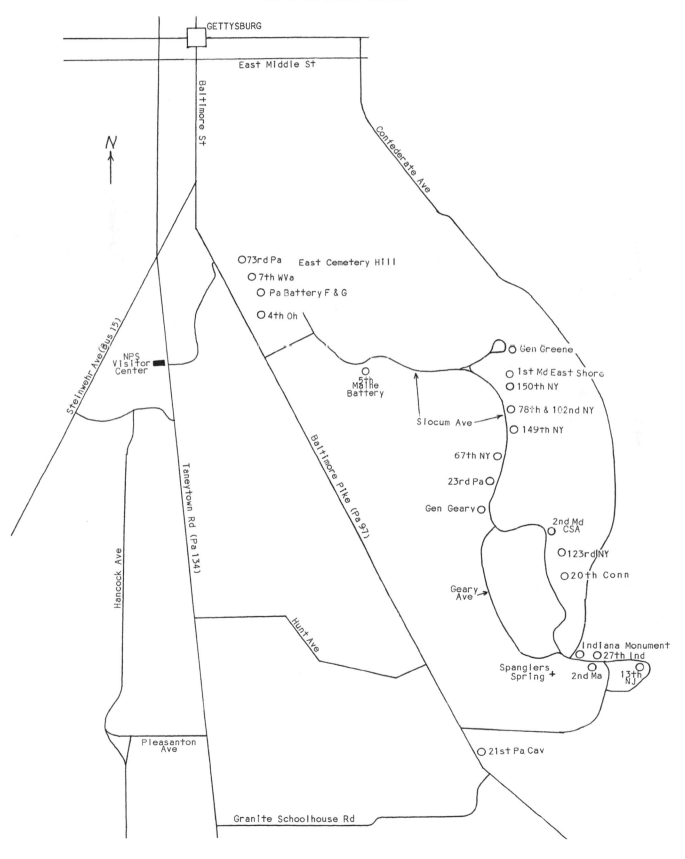

21st Pennsylvania Cavalry

The 21st Pennsylvania Cavalry was organized just prior to the battle of Gettysburg as part of the general mobilization to meet the threat of Lee's invasion of the state. One young Adams countian who had enlisted in Company B of the unit was George W. Sandoe. His army service was destined to be short-lived. On June 26, a portion of the Confederate infantry division of General Jubal Early entered the town of Gettysburg, the first Confederate force to do so. One of Early's brigadiers, John B. Gordon, sent out pickets to patrol the roads radiating out of town to the east and south. Elements of the 21st Pennsylvania Cavalry were also patrolling in the vicinity at that time. Private Sandoe and a comrade were riding cross country and as they approached the Baltimore Pike a scrub growth of bushes and trees masked the Confederate pickets from their sight. Coming out on the road they were ordered to halt. Sandoe's companion jumped his horse back over the fence and escaped. As Sandoe attempted to do the same, his horse fell. Recovering quickly he spurred the horse

onward, trying to escape the way he had come whereupon he was shot and killed. Just six days after enlisting in the Union army, and three days after being mustered into United States service, Private George Sandoe became the first casualty of war in the Gettysburg area.[1] He is buried today at the Mount Joy Church Cemetery, Mount Joy, Adams County.

The monuments to the 21st Pennsylvania Cavalry are located near the spot where Sandoe was killed.[2] The first was erected using the state appropriation and consists of a base supporting a highly polished granite ball inset with a sculpture of a horse's head. A year later, the veterans of the unit erected another monument within thirty yards of the state memorial. This one was paid for from funds they had privately raised. One possible explanation of why they would build a second monument so close to the first and so soon afterwards may rest with the fact that the newer monument contains the names of several of the officers of the unit. This was a practice not permitted by the state Monument Commission on any memorial built with state funds. This second monument was dedicated on October 4, 1894.

[1] Storrick, *Battle of Gettysburg,* p, 18.
[2] *Pennsylvania at Gettysburg,* 2:901–902.

REF

LOCATION: BALTIMORE PIKE
DEDICATED: OCTOBER 5, 1893
COST: $1500
SCULPTOR: EDWIN ELWELL
CONTRACTOR: JOHN FERGUSON
                MARBLE & GRANITE WORK
MATERIAL: CONNECTICUT GRANITE
SPECIFICATIONS: BASE–5′ SQ × 1′6″H
                2ND BASE–3′3″ SQ × 1′3″H
                DIE–3′3″ SQ × 3′H
                BALL–3′6″ DIA

13th New Jersey Infantry

The monument to the 13th New Jersey Infantry contains one of the finest bas relief carvings on the battlefield. It is located on a knoll overlooking Rock Creek, on the spot where the unit's colors stood on the morning of July 3 as is supported regiments attempting to drive the Confederates off of Culp's Hill.[1]

A meeting of the Veteran's Association of the 13th New Jersey in the fall of 1886 led to the formation of a monument committee. Over a thousand dollars was raised privately to supplement the state appropriation. The design, suggested by members of the unit, consists of a fully equipped Union soldier kneeling and aiming his rifle.[2] This was the second New Jersey regimental monument to be erected on the field and the first in which the New Jersey Monument Commission was involved.

[1] Toombs, *New Jersey Troops in the Gettysburg Campaign*, p. 342.
[2] *Report of the Gettysburg Battlefield Commission of New Jersey*, p. 21.

LOCATION: CARMAN AVENUE
DEDICATED: JULY 1, 1887
COST: $2000
DESIGNER: MEMBERS OF THE REGIMENT
CONTRACTOR: SMITH GRANITE COMPANY
MATERIAL: WESTERLY GRANITE
SPECIFICATIONS: 5′9″W × 2′10″W × 7′H
               THICKNESS AT TOP–2′
               BASE WEIGHT–8 TONS
               DIE WEIGHT–13 TONS

KLS

2nd Massachusetts Infantry

The small granite marker of the 2nd Massachusetts Infantry attracts little notice. Its importance rests in the fact that it was the first regimental monument of any type to be erected at Gettysburg.

To the men of the 2nd Massachusetts, the battle of Gettysburg consisted of an ill-fated charge across Spangler's Meadow to dislodge Confederate infantry from the Union defenses they had captured the evening before. About 10:00 A.M. of July 3, an aide to brigade commander Silas Colgrove rode up to Colonel Charles R. Mudge and delivered an order to charge the works in his front. Knowing such a charge to be suicide, Mudge questioned the aide who confirmed the order. Mudge replied, "Well, it is murder, but that's the order." Turning to his regiment he shouted "Up men; over the works. Forward. Double quick!"[1] The three hundred sixteen officers and men of the 2nd Massachusetts charged out of the woods and into the open meadow. They came under the fire of three Confederate regiments, two behind the stone wall in front and the other in the woods to their left. Before long they were forced to fall back under the heavy concentrated fire. The meadow was left littered with the regiment's casualties.[2] Among these was Colonel Mudge, shot dead while leading his men across the meadow.

In honor of the men of their unit that fell during the charge that day, the Veteran Association of the 2nd Massachusetts purchased a small plot of land from the Spangler farm on the edge of the meadow. Here, they proposed to place a small memorial. Designed by Joshua Haypold, it was erected in May, 1879 and bears an inscription relating to the unit's service at Gettysburg. On the back a plaque contains the names of the four officers and forty-one enlisted men of the regiment who lost their lives as a result of the action that day.

[1] Edwin B. Coddington, *The Gettysburg Campaign: A Study in Command,* (Dayton, Ohio: Press of Morningside Bookshop, 1979), p. 474; Bruce Catton, *The Army of the Potomac: Glory Road,* (Garden City, N.J.: Doubleday and Company, Inc., 1952), p. 307.

[2] Vanderslice, *Gettysburg Then and Now,* p. 235.

KLS

LOCATION: CARMAN AVENUE
DEDICATED: MAY 1879
DESIGNER: JOSHUA HAYPOLD
MATERIAL: BLAKE AND COMPANY FOUNDERS

27th Indiana Infantry

The 27th Indiana Infantry accompanied the 2nd Massachusetts across Spangler's Meadow in the attempt to drive the Confederates back from Culp's Hill. A small marker in the middle of the field marks the farthest point reached by the unit in its charge. This marker can be seen in the photo, just to the left of the main monument. Of the three hundred thirty-nine infantrymen who participated, nearly one-third of them would become casualties of the battle, including eight men who fell bearing the colors.

The monument to the unit "... a small, unpretentious granite shaft," was erected in 1885 on the site over which the left wing of the regiment passed in its assault.[1] The boulder underneath the monument was used during the battle to shelter some of the wounded of the regiment who fell during the charge.[2] A bronze plaque was attached on the back of the granite shaft in 1902 to correct the original inscription. At the top of the shaft is a red, five-pointed star, the symbol of the 1st Division, 12th Army Corps.

[1] Edmund R. Brown, *The Twenty-seventh Indiana Volunteer Infantry in the War of the Rebellion, 1861–1865, First Division, 12th and 20th Corps,* (Monticello, 1899), p. 403.

[2] Ibid., p. 404.

LOCATION: CARMAN AVENUE
                  (SPANGLER MEADOW)
DEDICATED: 1885
COST: $500
MATERIAL: BEDFORD LIMESTONE

KLS

Indiana State Memorial

The state of Indiana appropriated $3000 in March, 1885 for its regiments to erect suitable monuments on the field at Gettysburg. The sum allotted provided for little more than simple, unadorned markers. This fact was pointed out by many early guidebooks and histories. One, remarking on the simplicity of the state's regimental monuments, stated that "... there seems to have been no effort towards originality or impressiveness."[1] Following the 50th anniversary ceremonies in 1913, many Hoosiers who had visited the field expressed "mortification" at the style of Indiana's monuments in that "... they are not in keeping with what the government and other states have done ... to preserve the memory of the heroes who fell there."[2]

Another fifty-five years would pass before efforts were made to provide a more fitting monument to Indiana's soldiers at Gettysburg. In October of 1968 a Gettysburg Memorial Commission was appointed by the governor of Indiana to oversee the design and erection of a large state monument on the battlefield. A Gettysburg company, Codori Memorials, submitted a design the committee ultimately chose. It was built in the fall of 1970. The site selected was Spangler's Meadow, the place where the 27th Indiana had suffered such tremendous casualties. The twenty-eight thousand pound cenotaph consists of two ten-foot high pylons soaring on either side of the die. The terrace on which the monument was placed, the walkway, and two benches that flank the memorial are all made from Bedford, Indiana limestone. On July 1, 1971 the monument was formally dedicated.

[1] Vanderslice, *Gettysburg Then and Now*, p. 459.
[2] W. N. Pickerill, Compiler and Editor, *Indiana at the Fiftieth Anniversary of the Battle of Gettysburg: Report of the Fiftieth Anniversary Commission of the Battle of Gettysburg*, (n.c. n.p.: n.d.), p. 109.

LS

LOCATION: SPANGLER'S MEADOW
DEDICATED: JULY 1, 1971
COST: $17,000
DESIGNER: AL YEAGER
CONTRACTOR: CODORI MEMORIALS
MATERIAL: BARRE GRANITE
              BEDFORD LIMESTONE
SPECIFICATIONS: TWO 10' PYLONS
                     WEIGHT–28,000 POUNDS

The monument to the 20th Connecticut Infantry is of the same simple style as other monuments to Connecticut units on the field. The unit it honors played an unusual role in the battle. On the morning of July 2, the 20th was in position at the location of the monument, aiding in the construction of breastworks. Most of the 12th Corps was sent to the left of the Union line to aid in the fighting. A short while after they marched away, the Confederates attacked Culp's Hill capturing most of the abandoned Union defenses. As the 20th Connecticut arrived back in the area after dark, they found their position occupied by the enemy.

At dawn July 3, a planned counterattack to recapture the hill began with an artillery bombardment. The 20th Connecticut was advanced into the woods under orders to keep their brigade and divisional commanders informed of Confederate movements. These reports were then used to allow for more accurately obtaining the range for Union artillery, increasing the accuracy of the shellfire. This example of advanced artillery spotters, a common practice today, was one of the first times it was used in battle.[1]

Being close to the impact area of Union shellfire was not without risks. Coming in just over the heads of the men of the 20th, occasional shells fell short, either through misjudgements of range or defective fuses. Several casualties were sustained in this manner. When one shellburst over the unit cost a soldier both arms, Lt. Colonel William Wooster angrily sent back word to the battery commander that if it happened again he would pull his men out of line, face them about and charge his own guns.[2] A veteran of the unit later remarked that Wooster was just the sort of man to do this.

Years later when the monument to the 20th Connecticut was dedicated, George W. Warner, the man who had lost his arms in the shelling, was given the honor of unveiling the new regimental monument. A special pulley assembly, connected to the flag covering the monument, allowed Warner to pull the flag off by walking away with a rope tied around his waist.

[1] *War of the Rebellion: The Official Records of the Union and Confederate Armies*, Series 1, Volume XXVII, Part 1,

(Washington, D.C.: Government Printing Office, 1889), p. 793.

[2] Fairfax Downey, *The Guns At Gettysburg,* (New York: Collier Books, 1962) p. 136.

George W. Warner   *USMI*

REF

LOCATION: SOUTH SLOCUM AVENUE
DEDICATED: JULY 3, 1885
COST: $950
DESIGNER/CONTRACTOR: CURTIS & HUGHS

123rd New York Infantry

New York is well represented with regimental monuments on the slope of Culp's Hill. One of the most artistic is the one honoring the 123rd New York Infantry. Standing alongside the remains of breastworks recaptured from the Confederates by the unit on the morning of July 3, the monument features a large granite statue entitled "History Recording". Representing Clio, the muse of history, the statue is depicted writing the events of the battle on a large tablet.[1] Both the front and back faces of the shaft displays a bronze five-pointed star, symbol of the 12th Army Corps. A short distance out in front of the breastworks is a small reddish companion marker identifying the position of the skirmish line of the regiment.

[1] Vanderslice, *Gettysburg Then and Now*, pp. 289, 428.

REF

LOCATION: SOUTH SLOCUM AVENUE
DEDICATED: SEPTEMBER 4, 1888
COST: $4,000
SCULPTOR: J. G. HAMILTON
DESIGNER/CONTRACTOR: SMITH GRANITE
                                            COMPANY
MATERIAL: WESTERLY GRANITE
                    STANDARD BRONZE
SPECIFICATIONS: BASE–8'0"SQ
                            HEIGHT–18'2"
                            STATUE–2'3"SQ × 7'0"H
                            TABLETS–2'2" × 1'6"

2nd Maryland Infantry (Confederate States of America)

The only regimental monument on the battlefield built by a Confederate veteran's group is that of the 1st Maryland Battalion. The 1st Maryland was part of General George (Maryland) Steuart's brigade of General Edward Johnson's division, Richard Ewell's 2nd Corps. It participated in the successful assault and capture of the lightly defended Union positions on lower Culp's Hill the evening of July 2 and held the position until the entire Confederate line was repulsed before noon July 3.

In October 1884, the Board of Directors of the Gettysburg Battlefield Memorial Association granted permission to the survivors of the 1st Maryland to erect a monument indicating its position on the field.[1] It was not accomplished without controversy, as some Union veterans steadfastly opposed their former enemy's desire to honor their own dead. One concession the unit needed to make was to use the designation 2nd Maryland to avoid confusion with two Union regiments that fought in the vicinity with the same numeric designation.[2] The site chosen for the monument was the position occupied by the unit as they broke into the Union defenses on July 2. Nearby, the commander of the regiment was mortally wounded.

The monument consists of a tapered die topped by a highly polished granite ball. On the front of the die is a large bas relief carving of the Maryland state seal. Each of the four faces of the capstone has the Baltimore Cross as most of the men in the regiment were recruited in and around this city. The dedication took place in November of 1886 in the presence of a large number of onlookers in the audience including the former brigade commander, General Steuart. At the same time a small marker was placed approximately one hundred yards inside Union lines to represent the point reached by the unit during the morning's fighting on July 3.

[1] Vanderslice, *Gettysburg Then and Now*, p. 372.
[2] The other units were the 1st Maryland (Potomac Home Brigade) and the 1st Maryland (Eastern Shore).

LOCATION: SOUTH SLOCUM AVENUE
DEDICATED: NOVEMBER 19, 1886
COST: $1,000
DESIGNER/CONTRACTOR: STANDARD GRANITE
                                COMPANY
MATERIAL: HARDWICK GRANITE
SPECIFICATIONS: 5'4" SQ × 9'6"H

REF

John Geary Portrait Statue

The portrait statue of General John White Geary was erected on Culp's Hill in the area where his 'White Star' Division fought on the morning of July 3. His division was instrumental in repulsing the elements of the Confederate army that had gained a lodgement on the slopes of Culp's Hill the night before.

Geary was perhaps the largest general in the army. A huge man by the standards of the time, he was solidly built weighing between two hundred and two hundred fifty pounds and standing six-feet five and one-half inches tall. A lawyer and Civil Engineer by profession, Geary's most impressive accomplishments were political. He had established the postal service in the San Francisco area before the war, eventually serving as first mayor of the city. In 1856, he was appointed the territorial governor of Kansas at a time when the slavery issue was earning the territory the nickname 'Bleeding Kansas.' His unswerving antislavery views, legendary stubbornness, and violent temper resulted in numerous confrontations with proslavery forces and Geary's eventual resignation. Following distinguished military service in the Civil War, Geary served two consecutive terms as governor of Pennsylvania. Just three weeks after leaving office, the general died suddenly at the age of fifty-three.[1]

The statue of General Geary was authorized by the state of Pennsylvania as a tribute to his contribution both on and off the battlefield. Sculpted by J. Otto Schweizer the monument was placed on the field in the summer of 1915. The statue was never formally dedicated.

[1] Faust, *Encyclopedia of the Civil War,* p. 302; Warner, *Generals in Blue,* pp. 169-170; Paul Beers, "John W. Geary: A Profile," *Civil War Times Illustrated,* June 1970, pp. 11–16.

LS

LOCATION: NORTH SLOCUM AVENUE
COMPLETED: 1915
DEDICATED: NEVER
COST: $6,666
SCULPTOR: J. OTTO SCHWEIZER
CONTRACTOR: GORHAM MANUFACTURING
                            COMPANY
MATERIAL: STANDARD BRONZE

23rd Pennsylvania Infantry

One of the first regiments raised by the state of Pennsylvania for service in the Civil War was the 23rd Pennsylvania Infantry. Organized and recruited in the city of Philadelphia, they were nicknamed the Birney Zouaves after their first commander General David Birney. By the summer of 1863, the original Zouave uniform of the regiment had long since given way to the standard U.S. infantryman's uniform.

The monument to the 23rd Pennsylvania was erected in the summer of 1886 following a lengthy dispute with the Battlefield Memorial Association concerning the location.[1] Paid for by the regimental survivors, the die contains a complete history of the unit. The only real adornment on the shaft is the 6th Corps symbol, a Greek cross made from blue tiles; the color indicates the unit's affiliation with the 3rd Division. This division of the 6th Corps aided the 12th Corps in recapturing Culp's Hill on July 3. On either side of the cross are etchings of the unit's two battleflags: the one on the left, the National flag; on the right, the state flag. Originally a stack of highly polished granite cannonballs sat atop the monument.

Matthew Spence   REGIMENTAL HISTORY

When the state of Pennsylvania gave the unit money for monument construction, the Veteran's Association of the 23rd chose to use the appropriation to upgrade their existing one. At the suggestion of the unit's men, the cannonballs were removed from the top and replaced by a granite statue of a 'Birney Zouave.' Since the average age of the men was nineteen at the time of enlistment, the decision was made to portray the soldier as a boy. One of the unit's veterans, Matthew Spence, was selected to serve as the model. The statue depicts a youthful soldier partially clothed in the original Zouave uniform advancing up a slope at the position of 'trail arms'; he is under the fire of the enemy. The Culp's Hill area was wooded at the time of the battle and this was re-

flected by the broken tree stump that forms the base.[2] During the unveiling on June 12, 1888 in the presence of one hundred and twenty-nine regimental survivors, one veteran was heard to comment on how young the boy in the statue looked. Another veteran, standing alongside, replied, "We were young!"

[1] PaMC, Records pertaining to the 23rd Pennsylvania Infantry monument; William J. Wray, *History of the 23rd Pennsylvania Volunteer Infantry, Birney's Zouaves, Three Months and Three Years Service, Civil War, 1861–1865*, (Philadelphia, 1904), p. 271.

LS

LOCATION: NORTH SLOCUM AVENUE
BASE DEDICATED: AUGUST 6, 1886
STATUE DEDICATED: SEPTEMBER 12, 1889
COST: BASE–$850
     STATUE–$1500
CONTRACTOR (BASE)–BING AND CUNNINGHAM
CONTRACTOR (STATUE)–JOHN FERGUSON
  MARBLE & GRANITE WORKS
DESIGNER: STATUE–ONE OF THE REGIMENT
MATERIAL: QUINCY GRANITE
SPECIFICATIONS: BASE–4'6"SQ × 1'6"H
           STATUE–6'10"H

67th New York Infantry (1st Long Island Infantry)

Another of the 6th Corps units that aided in driving the Confederates away from Culp's Hill on the morning of July 3 was the 67th New York Infantry, known commonly as the 1st Long Island Infantry. Their monument designates the general area they held that morning. The most prominent feature on the memorial is a bronze plaque on the die symbolizing the completion of the soldier's work. Entitled "It is over", the plaque represents a Union infantryman standing amidst the debris of battle. In honor of those that have fallen in the cause, he stands at parade rest in the funeral position of 'Reverse Arms.'

The men of the 1st Long Island were typical of the vast majority of soldiers that made up the armies of North and South. Unlike the armies of Europe, few had received extensive formal military training, fewer still could be classed professional soldiers. By and large the bloodiest war this nation has ever fought was undertaken by citizen-soldiers. Rev. Thomas K. Beecher delivered the main oration at the dedication of the 1st Long Island monument in June 1888. In his speech he talked of the uniqueness of the American soldier that constituted the volunteer regiments:

"A million men at the call of our chief magistrate volunteered and became soldiers. This was the world's wonder. They fought their battles, buried their dead, went home with their wounded, and became citizens once more! This was and is the greatest wonder. The muster-in surprised mankind. The muster-out astounded them."[1]

[1] *New York at Gettysburg,* 2:560.

KLS

LOCATION: NORTH SLOCUM AVENUE
DEDICATED: JUNE 13, 1888
COST: $1,500
DESIGNER/CONTRACTOR: FREDERICK AND FIELD
MATERIAL: QUINCY GRANITE
           STANDARD BRONZE
SPECIFICATIONS: BASE–6'4"SQ
           HEIGHT–14'4"H
           BRONZE PLAQUE–2' × 2'2"

149th New York Infantry

In 1886, several former officers of the 149th New York Infantry visited the old battlefield at Gettysburg. In going over the Culp's Hill area where their unit had fought, they became concerned with the lack of markings in this crucial battle area. At the first regimental reunion following the visit, a monument committee was formed and designs discussed. The original monument the committee contracted was refused by the veterans after its completion, as they felt it varied too much from their specifications. Another company was selected, a second contract drawn up, and the monument was eventually erected.

When discussing designs for a second monument, one veteran suggested that a statue of the regimental color bearer, Sergeant William C. Lilly, be placed atop the base. A second suggestion was made to place a plaque depicting the breastwork defenses of the men of the 149th. These two ideas were incorporated into one, and the crude drawing of the committee members was sent to artist Edwin Forbes, who perfected the scene on canvas. This was then used in the actual modeling of the bronze plaque now present on the front of the monument.[1]

Entitled "Mending the flag under fire", it depicts an actual event during the fighting that day.

KLS

LOCATION: NORTH SLOCUM AVENUE
DEDICATED: SEPTEMBER 18, 1892
COST: $1,500
DESIGNER: (PLAQUE) EDWIN FORBES
SCULPTOR: (PLAQUE) RALPH COOK
CONTRACTOR: FRANCIS AND COMPANY
MATERIAL: BARRE GRANITE
SPECIFICATIONS: BASE–5'4" × 4'5"
                HEIGHT–11'8"
                RELIEF–2'6" × 2'0"
                TABLET–2'6" × 2'0"

Sergeant William C. Lilly   *REGIMENTAL HISTORY*

The unit's flag had been a present to the regiment and was much valued by the officers and men. In the intense fighting along the line, the flag of the 149th, planted on the breastworks, received over eighty bullet holes. At one point the staff was shot in two.[2] Color sergeant Lilly picked up the pieces and, under fire, used slats from a cracker box and straps from his knapsack to splice the staff together and replace the flag on the breastwork. It is this event that is portrayed on the plaque.[3]

Sergeant Lilly was mortally wounded at the battle of Wauhatchie, Tennessee the following October. As he was being moved to a field hospital in the rear, a driving rain pelted down. At his side, a wounded Confederate soldier lay in rags shivering uncontrollably from the intense cold and dampness. Despite great pain and loss of blood, Lilly shared his small blanket with this man, a former enemy.[4] It was this compassion and nobility, as well as bravery, that the unit wished to honor in their monument.

[1] *New York at Gettysburg*, 3:1019.

[2] Ibid., p. 1020; George K. Collins, *Memoirs of the One Hundred Forty-ninth Regiment New York Volunteer Infantry, 3rd Brig., 2d Div., 12th and 20th A.C.*, (Syracuse: the author, 1891), p. 150.

[3] *New York at Gettysburg*, 3:1019.

[4] Collins, *Memoirs of the One Hundred Forty-ninth Regiment New York*, pp. 376-377.

REGIMENTAL HISTORY

78th and 102nd New York Infantry

One of the finest carved granite statues on the battlefield is the kneeling infantryman on the monument to the 78th and 102nd New York Infantries at Culp's Hill. Both units had suffered heavy casualties prior to the battle and were considerably understrength on July 2 and 3 as they defended the hill. The 78th New York had less than two hundred officers and men, while the 102nd brought approximately two hundred fifty to Gettysburg. The following summer the two units were formally consolidated and the remainder of the war fought together as one. When the question of a monument at Gettysburg arose, the decision was made to combine their individual state appropriation.

The monument represents a Union infantryman defending a log and stone breastwork, similar to that which existed on parts of this hill during the battle.

On his right side is a cartridge box, unhooked so that he has easy access to the contents. His capbox on front of his belt is also unhooked, ready to provide the percussion cap necessary to fire the next round. His canteen and haversack complete the accoutrements.

One additional feature, often overlooked, is the illusion of the lion's head contained in the stone wall. At first glance, all that will appear in view are the rocks and logs that constitute the wall, but at the middle stone of the wall, just underneath the soldier's left hand, are the lightly carved features of the lion. The lower log appears to resemble the paw of the lion. This symbolizes the courage and bravery of the men defending the breastworks that day. In the winter of 1987, after nearly a century on the field, the statue was smashed by vandals.

DWM

LOCATION: NORTH SLOCUM AVENUE
DEDICATED: JULY 2, 1888
COST: $3,000
SCULPTOR: R. D. BARR
DESIGNER/CONTRACTOR: SMITH GRANITE
         COMPANY
MATERIAL: WESTERLY GRANITE
    STANDARD BRONZE
SPECIFICATIONS: BASE–8'5"L × 5'8"W
      BRONZE PALM BRANCH–2'0"

150th New York Infantry

The 150th New York Infantry, nicknamed the 'Dutchess County Regiment,' has one of the largest monuments on Culp's Hill. Built using the state appropriation and supplemented by an additional $3,000 raised in Dutchess county, the monument has more symbolism than any other on the field.

Designed to represent a 'tower of invincible strength,' it is composed of thirteen layers of stone. The number is emblematic of the nation's birth, unity, and stability. The stacked nature of the stone, with each holding the other in place, was to signifiy the unity, love, and mutual respect of the officers and men of the regiment. A bronze plate contains the names of each of the unit's men who lost their lives during the battle. Above the plate, a bronze, en-

twined laurel wreath and oak leaf was meant to symbolize the crowning of the citizen-soldier. On the front, underneath the plaque detailing the history of the regiment, is a border of state and national escutcheons with the New York seal behind the seal of the United States to indicate the supremacy of nation over state.[1]

Dedicated on September 17, 1889, the monument was unveiled by the daughter of the 150th's Colonel. The huge flag used to drape the memorial was the same flag raised over Atlanta, after General Sherman captured the city.[2]

[1] *New York at Gettysburg*, 3:1024.
[2] Ibid., p. 1025.

LOCATION: NORTH SLOCUM AVENUE
DEDICATED: SEPTEMBER 17, 1889
COST: $4,400
SCULPTOR: GEORGE E. BISSELL
DESIGNER/CONTRACTOR: VAN WYCK AND
                       COLLINS
MATERIAL: QUINCY GRANITE
           STANDARD BRONZE
SPECIFICATIONS: BASE–10'SQ
                 HEIGHT–23'8"
                 TABLETS–2' × 4'9"

FWH

1st Maryland Infantry (Eastern Shore)

Maryland, being a border state during the Civil War, had soldiers fighting in both armies at Gettysburg. The 1st Eastern Shore Maryland Infantry was one of the five regiments that this state contributed to the Army of the Potomac at Gettysburg. Their monument is the most artistic of the five Maryland monuments on the field. On the front of the stone is a bas relief sculpture of a Union infantryman lying behind a rock. During the morning battle of July 3 in this vicinity, the 1st Eastern Shore defended the breastworks at the site of the monument.

KLS

LOCATION: NORTH SLOCUM AVENUE
DEDICATED: OCTOBER 25, 1888
COST: $1,000
DESIGNER/CONTRACTOR: FREDERICK AND FIELD

George S. Greene Portrait Statue

The portrait statue of General George Sears Greene honors a man who was the oldest field commander in the Army of the Potomac. At the age of sixty-two, Green led his brigade of thirteen hundred fifty New Yorkers into battle at Gettysburg on July 2. When most of the Union 12th Corps was pulled off the hill to assist in bolstering the beleaguered left end of the Union battle line, Greene's brigade remained behind. Throughout that long evening his regiments held the summit of Culp's Hill against a force of the enemy that outnumbered his three to one. His efforts served to protect the vital Baltimore Pike supply line, left essentially unprotected by the departure of the 12th Corps.

Following the war, Greene resumed his profession as a Civil Engineer. He led a full and active life, often returning to the scene of his greatest military moment for veteran's reunions and monument dedications. At the General's death in 1899, a two-ton boulder was taken from the top of Culp's Hill and moved to Warwick, Rhode Island for placement over his grave, fulfilling a request he had made. Nearly ten years later, the State of New York chose to make Greene the third commander of New York troops to be honored with a portrait statue on the field. Standing on top of the hill Greene defended that day, the statue gazes down the slope, pointing in the direction the Confederate breakthrough took place that evening.

LOCATION: SUMMIT OF CULP'S HILL
DEDICATED: SEPTEMBER 26, 1907
COST: $6,863
SCULPTOR: R. HINTON PERRY
CONTRACTOR: BUREAU BROTHERS
                         BRONZE FOUNDERS
MATERIAL: STANDARD BRONZE

DWM

FWH

5th Maine Artillery

Just southwest of Culp's Hill is a small rise of ground known today as Steven's Knoll, named after the commander of the 5th Maine Battery, Captain Greenleaf T. Stevens. Using this position, the six smooth bore Napoleon guns of the battery had a commanding field of fire at any attacking column. On the evening of July 2, the value of the position was made apparent when two Confederate brigades attacked East Cemetery Hill in the early evening. Canister fired from Steven's guns played an important role in helping to repulse the Confederates.

The monument consists of a highly polished red beach granite die. The color of the stone is the traditional color of the artillery branch. At the top is a polished globe of black Addison granite representing a cannonball. A bas relief carving of a Napoleon with three artillerymen serving it is on the face of the monument. One man is adjusting the elevation screw in preparation for the next shot. The second

artilleryman "thumbs the vent," a necessary practice while loading to prevent air from getting into the vent causing a flareup of any burning powder embers. The third cannoneer loads the projectile down the tube.

One young private, temporarily assigned to the battery, was wounded while serving the guns during an artillery duel on the evening of July 2. John F. Chase had a Confederate case shot explode in front of him. Forty-eight pieces hit Chase, critically injuring him. With a shattered left arm, damaged eye and numerous other wounds, it seemed impossible for him to survive long. Two days later Chase was being transported for burial. The wagon his body was on hit a bump, jolting him back into consciousness. The driver was shocked to hear one of his 'passengers' ask "Did we win?" Chase was taken to a field hospital where his wounds were cleaned, examined, and pronounced fatal. To everyone's great surprise, John Chase survived. As one of the earliest battlefield guides, he escorted parties around the field on which he had sustained such terrible wounds.[1]

[1] Gettysburg Battlefield Monument Commission of Maine, *Maine at Gettysburg: Report of the Maine Commissioners, Prepared by the Executive Committee,* (Portland, Maine: The Lakeside Press, 1898), p. 93.

REF

LOCATION: STEVEN'S KNOLL
DEDICATED: OCTOBER 3, 1889
MATERIAL: HALLOWELL GRANITE
         RED BEACH GRANITE
         ADDISON GRANITE
SPECIFICATIONS: BASE–5'4"SQ × 1'8"H
              PLINTH–4'SQ × 2'4"H
              DIE–3'SQ × 6'H
              BALL–2'8"DIA

4th Ohio Infantry

The monument to the 4th Ohio Infantry stands on East Cemetery Hill at the spot where the regiment was sent in to aid in repulsing the attack of Hay's and Hoke's Confederate brigades at dusk on July 2. A smaller monument along the Emmitsburg Road honors Companies G and I at the location where they skirmished with the Confederates in the afternoon and evening of July 2.

A unique feature of these memorials is the material they were constructed of, a substance called "White Bronze." This whitish-blue metal was developed in the 1870's as a more durable alternative to pure bronze and at a somewhat cheaper price than carved granite. White bronze was basically zinc combined with scant amounts of nickle, tin, and copper. The company that marketed the product advertised the alloy as one that would never blacken or grow dingy with age as true bronze did. Moss could not grow or adhere to its surface and it would never chip or crumble like granite. The Veteran's Association of the 4th Ohio decided to use White Bronze in their Gettysburg monument.

The design chosen was the work of Peter B. Laird of the Monumental Bronze Company of Bridgeport, Connecticut and was apparently used several times.[1] It consists of a lower base cast to resemble rough hewn granite and an ornately carved second base. On the die is a complete history of the regiment including the names of the men who were killed or wounded in this battle. The capstone contains bas reliefs on each of its four faces. These include the state seal of Ohio, a stack of muskets with fixed bayonets, a pile of war materials topped by an eagle, and a series of battleflags. A tall shaft supporting a three hundred pound statue of a soldier at parade rest was originally set upon the base. This part was removed in 1976 because the heavy weight was causing stress cracks to appear at the base. One drawback of the white bronze, not apparent at the time of dedication, was its lack of strength. At the time of its dismantling, the monument was leaning 7° and was in great danger of toppling.

Shortly after the 4th Ohio Infantry dedicated their monument, the Gettysburg Battlefield Memorial Association's Board of Directors set specific regulations governing monument construction. Spurred on by dissatisfaction with the appearance of the white bronze of the 4th Ohio monument, the Board ruled that all future monuments at Gettysburg would be required to be made of granite or pure bronze.

[1] Monuments similar in design to that of the 4th Ohio were built at the Riverview Cemetery in Baldwinsville, New York, and Woodlawn Cemetery in Syracuse.

GNMP

LOCATION: EAST CEMETERY HILL
DEDICATED: SEPTEMBER 14, 1887
COST: $2,500
DESIGNER: PETER B. LAIRD
CONTRACTOR: MONUMENTAL BRONZE
              COMPANY
BUILT BY: W. N. MILLER, DEATRICH, & RUMNER
MATERIAL: WHITE BRONZE
SPECIFICATIONS: 1ST BASE–7'1/4"SQ × 1'9"H
                 2ND BASE–6'6"SQ × 2'9"H
                 DIE–5'9"SQ × 2'6"H
                 SHAFT–30 3/4"SQ × 9'5"H
                 CAP–31"SQ × 28½"H
                 STATUE–16 1/4"SQ × 6'2"H
                 TOTAL HEIGHT–28'5 1/2"

1st Pennyslvania Light Artillery Battery F & G

Rickett's Battery F, 1st Pennsylvania Light Artillery, was combined with Battery G a few weeks before the battle of Gettysburg in order to form a complete six gun battery from two understrength ones. At Gettysburg, the combined batteries under Captain R. Bruce Ricketts took position on the afternoon of July 2. They completed the construction of the gun emplacements (lunettes), begun earlier in the day, and prepared to resist any Confederate attack. When the attack finally came at dusk, sweeping across the valley towards the hill, Rickett's gunners fired case shot and canister at the advancing enemy. Eventually every round of canister would be used up as the Confederates charged up the slope, sweeping towards the guns. Here a fierce hand-to-hand battle took place as the gunners struggled to protect their guns using pistols, handspikes, and rammers.

The main face of the monument contains a bas relief of one of the unit's 3-inch Ordnance Rifles with the gun's Number 1 and Number 3 cannoneers in position awaiting the discharge. The job of Number 1 was to sponge the barrel and ram the charge to the base of the tube. Number 3's general responsibility was to hold his thumb on the vent during loading to keep oxygen from entering the tube. Artillery pieces were normally served by five to seven men, although drills were practiced enabling guns to be worked by as few as two men. In situations such as the close fighting that characterized this position on the second evening of the battle, less than complete gun crews may have been a common sight.

REF

LOCATION: EAST CEMETERY HILL
DEDICATED: JULY 2, 1894
COST: $3,000
DESIGNER/CONTRACTOR: SMITH GRANITE
                COMPANY
MATERIAL: BLUE WESTERLY GRANITE
SPECIFICATIONS: 11'L × 3'W × 9'H

7th West Virginia Infantry

West Virginia formally gained admission to the United States on June 20, 1863. On that day, several regiments were marching north with the Army of the Potomac in search of the Confederate army. One of those regiments, the 7th West Virginia Infantry, greeted the news with as much ceremony as could be mustered given the tensions of the moment. They would enter the battle of Gettysburg with the only American flag on the field with the appropriate number of stars. Apparently one jubilant mountaineer 'borrowed' a star from the flag of a neighboring unit, the 14th Indiana, and had sewn it onto one of the stripes of his unit's flag.

During the Confederate assault on East Cemetery Hill, the 7th West Virginia carried their flag into battle. The unit helped to drive the Confederate attackers away from the beleaguered guns of Rickett's and Weidrich's batteries. Today their monument stands on the location from which they drove the Confederates. It features the statue of a Union infantryman in full winter uniform, standing eternally on watch for signs of another movement against the hill.

On the back of the monument is the slogan "Sons of the Mountains," beneath which is the badge of the 7th West Virginia Veteran's Association, a ribbon holding a badge cut in the trefoil symbol of the 2nd Army Corps. The horseshoe with statement "We Have Crossed the Mountains" is the Spottswood Award, named for one of Virginia's colonial leaders, Lt. Governor Alexander Spottswood. He was instrumental in encouraging settlement in the western part of Virginia. In 1716 Spottswood led an expedition to the crest of the Blue Ridge, formally taking possession of the region. His travelling companions formed an organization named "Knights of the Golden Horseshoe". Later, Spottswood awarded people going west with a horseshoe, some of which were set with jewels. The members of the 7th West Virginia, descendants of those Spottswood had encouraged to migrate west, placed this award on their monument.

LOCATION: EAST CEMETERY HILL
DEDICATED: SEPTEMBER 28, 1898
COST: $500 +

LS

73rd Pennsylvania Infantry

The 73rd Pennsylvania Infantry also participated in the repulse of the Confederates on East Cemetery Hill on July 2. Lying in reserve in the Evergreen Cemetery, they rushed out through the cemetary gateway to help drive the Confederates away from Rickett's and Weidrich's batteries. Engaging the enemy hand-to-hand, they succeeded in repulsing the Confederates.

The most interesting feature on the monument is a highly detailed bronze plaque. This represents the 73rd's charge out of the cemetery. In the background, the Cemetery Gatehouse is present; the same one that stands today. In the foreground, the fight for the cannon is in progress as the regiment charges in. It very accurately depicts the action that occurred on this part of the field that evening.

REF

LOCATION: EAST CEMETERY HILL
DEDICATED: SEPTEMBER 12, 1889
COST: $2183
SCULPTOR: ALEXANDER M. CALDER
CONTRACTOR: GILES, MCMICHAEL & COMPANY
          GRANITE AND FLAGSTONE YARD
MATERIAL: QUINCY GRANITE
         STANDARD BRONZE
SPECIFICATIONS: 1ST BASE–6'SQ × 1'6"H
         1ST DIE–4'9"SQ × 2'7 1/2"H
         PLINTH–4'11"SQ × 1'H
         2ND DIE–4'2"SQ TAPERS TO 4'SQ
         × 4'9"H
         PLAQUES–3'4" × 2'0"
         CAP 4'1"SQ × 3'3"H
         CRESCENT–1'6" × 1'4" × 0'6"

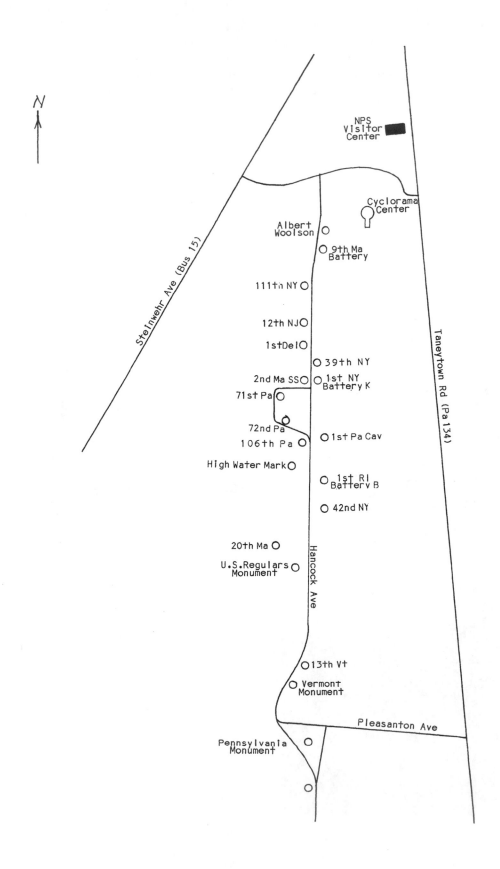

Vermont State Memorial

The state of Vermont was the first to build a large state memorial at Gettysburg, the purpose of which was to honor all of her citizens that participated in the battle. The Vermont Monument Commission received designs submitted from all parts of the country from which they chose the one embodied in the present memorial.

A massive base supports a large die, the front of which has a bas relief carving of the state's Coat of Arms. The remaining three faces give brief accounts of each of the Vermont organization's services at Gettysburg: L. A. Grant's 1st Vermont Brigade, George Stannard's 2nd Vermont Brigade, the 1st Vermont Cavalry, and the Vermont Sharpshooters.

A fifty-five foot high Corinthian column is topped by an eleven-foot portrait statue of General George Stannard, commander of one of the Vermont brigades during the battle. The task of sculpting the general was difficult; a good photographic profile of Stannard did not exist. The sculptor, Karl Gerhardt, worked on a plaster model of the head which he submitted to Mrs. Stannard and the General's daughters who felt it was excellent.[1] Stannard is portrayed as missing his right arm, a war loss that he sustained after this battle. The entire monument was created to honor the valor and sacrifice of Vermont's citizens throughout the war. Stannard's missing arm, it was felt, would underscore the sacrifices that helped preserve the Union.[2]

[1] Vermont Gettysburg Monuments Commission, *Report of the Vermont Commissioners 1890 (Including the Speeches and Poem at the Dedication) October 9, 1889*, (Burlington: The Free Press Assocation, 1890, p. 7.

[2] Ibid.

FWH

FWH

LOCATION: HANCOCK AVENUE
DEDICATED: OCTOBER 9, 1889
COST: $11,750
SCULPTOR: KARL GERHARDT
DESIGNER/CONTRACTOR: HENRY BONNARD
                              BRONZE CO.
MATERIAL: GRANITE
               STANDARD BRONZE
SPECIFICATIONS: COLUMN–55'H
                    STATUE—11'H

13th Vermont Infantry

The 13th Vermont Infantry monument consists of a set of quite detailed plaques relating the history of the unit in this battle and the war. Thirteen bronze stars surround the top of the base, symbolizing the common heritage of the nation. The portrait statue atop the base is unique because it honors a junior officer, Lieutenant Stephen F. Brown of Company K. The story behind the honoring of a lieutenant is an interesting one. One of the few nine month regiments in the Army of the Potomac, the 13th was within three weeks of the end of their term of service when this battle was fought. With the rest of Stannard's Vermont Brigade, they were involved in the army's forced march to the field. Food was in short supply; the constant hard marching wore out shoes; men passed out from intense heat, hunger and thirst. In order to prevent straggling and the resulting weakening of the army, orders were issued forbidding the men from leaving the ranks except during halts. Guards were placed at key points along the route to insure compliance. Near Frederick, Maryland, the men of the 13th Vermont passed one such guarded point: a well. Many men were suffering greatly from thirst and the senselessness of the situation became too much for Lieutenant Brown. Taking the canteens of his men, he and Private Oliver Parazo went to the well where they were accosted by the guard: "You can't get water here. Gainst orders." Brown replied "Damn your orders," gave the guard his name, rank, and regiment, and proceeded to fill the canteens.[1] This action led to his arrest and the symbol of command, his sword, was taken from him.

On the afternoon of July 3, the Vermont Brigade prepared to meet the advance of General George Pickett's Confederate division. The commander of the 13th Vermont, Lt. Colonel William D. Munson, went to General Stannard to intercede on Brown's behalf. As a result, Brown was released from arrest and allowed to resume command. Unfortu-nately, his sword had been sent to the rear, so the Lieutenant grabbed the nearest available weapon, a camp hatchet. As Pickett's men crossed the fields, they veered north, away from the Vermonters. Seeing Pickett's flank vulnerable to attack, Stannard ordered his brigade to swing into the fields to hit them. The 13th Vermont became the regiment the rest of the brigade pivoted on. Lt. Brown's company charged into the mass of Confederates and he spotted an enemy officer nearby. Rushing up, he seized the officer with his left hand, swung the hatchet threateningly over the man's head, and demanded his surrender.[2] The Confederate was so startled at the audacious, hatchet-wielding Brown, he turned his sword and loaded pistol over to the young Vermonter.

In 1896, the Veteran's Association of the 13th Vermont formed a monument committee to design a suitable memorial for the field. James Scully, the man who had served as the pivot on which Stannard's brigade turned in their flanking movement, suggested the design finally chosen.[3] The original model submitted to the War Department depicted Brown

LOCATION: HANCOCK AVENUE
DEDICATED: OCTOBER 19, 1899
COST: $4,166
SCULPTOR: F. MOYNEHAM
DESIGNER: JAMES B. SCULLY
CONTRACTOR: BASE—J. H. WALLING CO
      STATUE—GORHAM
         MANUFACTURING
MATERIAL: RYEGATE GRANITE
      STANDARD BRONZE

LS

with the hatchet in hand as he appeared during the fight. This design was not approved as the officials believed that it commemorated disobedience of orders, a poor example to set for future generations. The final design depicts Brown holding the captured sword in hand while the hatchet appears on the ground under his right foot. Stephen Brown personally posed for his statue and both hatchet and sword were modeled from the actual ones.[4]

At the dedication of the monument, the major participants in the event, Stephen Brown, Oliver Parazo, James Scully and Colonel Munson, were all in attendance. Towering above them on top of the state monument was the statue of the late General Stannard. The memorial they unveiled that day honors the great humanity, high moral courage, and conspicuous bravery, not only of Stephen Brown, but all the men of the regiment.[5] Five years later, the marking of the positions of the 13th Vermont was completed with the erection of three small markers noting the positions of the regiment during its fight with Pickett's men that July afternoon.

[1] Storrick, *Battle of Gettysburg*, p. 53.
[2] Ralph O. Sturdevant and Eli N. Peck, *Pictorial History Thirteenth Regiment Vermont Volunteers, War of 1861–1865*, (Burlington: Regimental Assocation, 1910), p. 808.
[3] Ibid.
[4] Ibid., p. 806.
[5] Ibid.

United States Regulars Monument

The Army of the Potomac and the Army of Northern Virginia were composed primarily of volunteer units raised in individual states. The professional, standing army of the United States was quite small prior to the war and formed only a very small part of the Union army at Gettysburg. These regulars were distributed in twenty-one artillery batteries, eleven infantry regiments, and four cavalry regiments. One hundred seventy-one regular soldiers lost their lives in this battle, nine hundred twenty-three were wounded, and two hundred eighty-one were listed as missing in action.

The regular infantry regiments were largely combined in two 5th Corps brigades under the command of Colonel Sidney Burbank and Colonel Hannibal Day. They participated in the fighting on the evening of July 2 in the Wheatfield/Devil's Den area. Regular Army artillery batteries and cavalry regiments served interspersed with their volunteer counterparts in all corps and on all parts of the battlefield, greatly contributing to the battle's outcome. The locations where each fought are marked today with identical granite stones with bronze plaques detailing each unit's battle history. Above each plaque is the Great Seal of the United States.

It was long felt that something more should be done to honor the men who served in the Regular Army units. The present U.S. Regular's monument on Cemetery Ridge grew out of that desire. Consisting of a tall, obelisk shaft mounted on a massive granite base, the monument is one of the largest on the battlefield. The main die contains bronze plaques, listing each regular regiment and battery that served here, along with the name of the commander. On the patio wall surrounding the monument are bronze United States Seals and Crests. On Memorial Day, 1909, the obelisk was dedicated by President William Howard Taft in the presence of a large contingent of Regular Army soldiers on hand to honor their predecessors.

LOCATION: HANCOCK AVENUE
DEDICATED: MAY 30, 1909
CONTRACTOR: VAN AMRINGE GRANITE
MATERIAL: MT. AIRY GRANITE

FWH

20th Massachusetts Infantry

The men who fought at Gettysburg and survived the war often searched for unique and meaningful designs to incorporate in their regimental monuments. In the one erected to honor the men of the 20th Massachusetts, one can readily see its uniqueness. This unit included men from throughout the entire state, yet was recruited and organized in the city of Roxbury. Through nearly two years of war, the 20th fought bravely, suffering numerous casualties. At Gettysburg, participating in the latter phases of the evening battle of July 2 and in repulsing Pickett's Charge on July 3, forty-four members of the unit would lay down their lives for the Union.

One of these casualties was the third Colonel of the regiment, Paul Joseph Revere, the grandson of the famous patriot of Revolutionary War fame. Fighting in the defense of the nation his grandfather had helped bring into existence, Colonel Revere was mortally wounded by shellfire during the attack of Anderson's Confederate division the evening of July 2.[1]

Another of the casualties of the 20th was their young Lieutenant, Sumner Paine. At the onset of war in 1861, Paine had just been admitted to Harvard at the tender age of sixteen. As the war continued, the scholarly life paled in comparison with a young man's vision of the spectacle and grandeur of battle. Shortly before his eighteenth birthday, he received a commission as a 2nd Lieutenant in the 20th. Just two months later, still imbued with the concept of war as a great adventure, young Paine arrived at Gettysburg with his regiment. As Pickett's men swept towards his position, Lieutenant Paine was out in front of his company. A bullet shattered his leg. Sinking to one knee he urged his men to continue on. "Isn't this glorious" he was heard to say. Just then a Confederate shell hit Paine, killing him instantly.[2]

The deaths of Colonel Revere, Lieutenant Paine, and many other comrades, led to a desire to create a special memorial in their honor. For years, a large conglomerate boulder was a prominent landmark on a popular playground in Roxbury. It was decided to transport this eighteen ton rock to Gettysburg to forever mark the site where the soldiers of the 20 Massachusetts who ". . . had once played around [the rock] fought so gallantly."[3] A bronze descriptive tablet on the base was the gift of Colonel Revere's daughter, Mrs. Nathaniel Thayer.[4]

[1] George A. Bruce, *The Twentieth Regiment of Massachusetts Volunteer Infantry, 1861–1865,* (Boston: Houghton-Mifflin Company, 1906), p. 283. Later on in the same source it states that Colonel Revere was struck by shellfire during the cannonade preceding Pickett's Charge, dying two days later. p. 296. The July 2 date was selected as more accurate as this was also stated in the official battle report of the 20th Massachusetts (OR, Series 1, Volume 27, Part 1, p. 445.

[2] Gregory A. Coco, *On the Bloodstained Field,* (Hollidaysburg, Pa.: The Wheatfield Press, 1987), p. 31.

[3] Vanderslice, *Gettysburg Then and Now,* p. 301, 411.

[4] Bruce, *The Twentieth Regiment,* p. viii.

LOCATION: HANCOCK AVENUE
DEDICATED: JUNE 1886
COST: $500
DESIGNER/CONTRACTOR: SMITH GRANITE CO.
MATERIAL: WESTERLY GRANITE
                CONGLOMERATE STONE

LS

40th and 42nd New York Infantries

Factional party politics played a role in the existence of two regiments that have monuments on the field at Gettysburg today, the 40th and 42nd New York Infantries. Identified as the party of secession by many northerners of the time, the Democratic party struggled to regain some semblance of power in the aftermath of the South's break from the Union. New York City was a traditional stronghold of the party and in that city several rival Democratic factions existed.

LOCATION: VALLEY OF DEATH
DEDICATED: JULY 2, 1888
COST: $2,225
SCULPTOR: R. D. BARR
CONTRACTOR: GRANITE—SMITH GRANITE CO.
     BRONZE—BUREAU BROTHERS
MATERIAL: HALLOWELL GRANITE
     WESTERLY GRANITE
SPECIFICATIONS: 7'0"L × 4'0"W × 6'10"H
     TABLET—1'1 3/4"SQ

DWM

At the beginning of the war, Mayor Fernando Wood, chairman of the city's Union Defense Committee, called upon his element of the party, nicknamed the "Mozart Faction," to raise and equip a regiment for service in the war.[1] In their haste to get a unit into the field, men from all sources were accepted and, as finally consitituted, the 40th New York Infantry contained only four companies from New York City. Four more companies were from Massachusetts, while the remaining two were from the city of Philadelphia.[2] Fighting in the Valley of Death below Little Round Top, July 2, the "Mozarts" aided in preventing the Confederate capture of the

LS

LOCATION: HANCOCK AVENUE
DEDICATED: SEPTEMBER 24, 1891
COST: $8,500
SCULPTOR: JOHN J. BOYLE
CONTRACTOR: GRANITE—JOHN HANNA
MATERIAL: QUINCY GRANITE
     STANDARD BRONZE
SPECIFICATIONS: BASE—12'SQ
     HEIGHT—27'10"
     TEEPEE—6'1" × 16'
     STATUE—7'H

hill. Their monument, cleverly carved to depict a soldier kneeling behind a boulder, is often overlooked as it blends in with the numerous large boulders in the valley, many of which sheltered the men of the unit that day. Another unique feature of the monument centers around the fact that it is the only regimental monument on the field erected using appropriations from two states to complete it. In addition to the $1500 New York appropriation, the Veteran's Association also applied for and was granted the $500 Massachusetts appropriation.

About the same time that Mayor Wood's faction was involved in organizing the 40th New York, a larger, more powerful Democratic faction was determined not to be left out. The Tammany Society became involved in recruiting a regiment which fought near the Copse of Trees the afternoon of July 3. Perhaps the most controversial regimental monument, it features a large bronze wigwam and a statue of an Indian warrior, Chief Tamenend. Tamenend was the leading chief of the Delaware Indians when the colony of Pennsylvania was originally settled. His bravery, skill, courage, and diplomacy were legendary. Tammany Societies were formed in several areas, the one in New York dating from 1786.[3] Originally a patriotic and charitable organization, it even-

tually became associated with party politics. When the society organized the 42nd New York it quickly became known as the "Tammany regiment" and its members were called "Braves."[4]

The sculpture atop the monument contains a quite detailed depiction of Indian life and is the most expensive sculpture on any regimental monument. Much of its cost was underwritten by the Tammany Society just as they had underwritten the cost of raising the regiment in 1861. The presence of this statue has frequently been criticized by many due to its theme. Even as it was being erected, many felt that it would ". . . lead to the misconception as to Indians participating in the battle.[5]

[1] Frederick C. Floyd, *History of the Fortieth (Mozart) Regiment New York Volunteers*, (Boston: F. H. Gilson Company, 1909), p. 30; *New York at Gettysburg*, 1:297.

[2] Floyd, *History of the Fortieth New York*, pp. 37–38.

[3] George P. Donehoo, *Indian Villages and Place Names in Pennsylvania*, (Harrisburg; The Telegraph Press, 1928), pp. 221–222.

[4] Craven, *Sculptures at Gettysburg*, p. 37.

[5] John M. Vanderslice, *Gettysburg Then and Now*, (New York: G. W. Dillingham, 1899; reprint ed., Dayton: Morningside Bookshop Press, 1983), p. 428.

Battery B, 1st Rhode Island Artillery

Rhode Island was represented in the battle of Gettysburg by three artillery batteries and one infantry regiment. When the state legislature discussed the matter of appropriating funds for monument construction, a strong movement developed to honor all Rhode Island units with one massive monument. After investigating what other states had done, the decision was made to erect a special monument for each unit.

The veterans of Captain T. Fred Brown's Battery B, 1st Rhode Island Artillery used their appropriation to erect a monument at the site of the battery's position during the cannonade of July 3 that preceded Pickett's Charge. Brown's battery first went into action at Gettysburg on the afternoon of July 2. Positioned in the open field between the Copse of

LOCATION: HANCOCK AVENUE
DEDICATED: OCTOBER 13, 1886
COST: $500
DESIGNER/CONTRACTOR: JOHN FLAHERTY
MATERIAL: WESTERLY GRANITE
SPECIFICATIONS: BASE–3'8"SQ × 15"H
                SHAFT–3 ½"H
                OVERALL HEIGHT–7 ½'
                WEIGHT–4 1/2 TONS

FWH

Trees and the Codori buildings, they were overrun and their guns captured when Wright's Georgia brigade attacked through the farm that evening. Fortunately a quick Union counterattack, spearheaded by the 106th Pennsylvania, recaptured the guns before they could be removed.

On July 3, the battery was in the hottest spot in the afternoon cannonade. Losses from July 2 had reduced the battery to the point where just four guns could be worked. As these four replied to the Confederate cannons across the valley, projectiles exploded all around. One of their guns was being loaded at the instant a Confederate shell hit the muzzle face and exploded. Private William Jones, holding the rammer in his job of Number 1, was killed instantly as a shell fragment tore through the side of his head. Beside him, Number 2, Private Alfred Gardner, had started to insert the next round when the shell hit tearing his left arm off. He died shouting "Glory to God! I am happy! Hallelujah!" The two remaining gunners, Sergeant Albert Straight and Corporal Joseph M. Dye, tried to finish loading. Dye thumbed the vent while the Sergeant attempted to load the round. The dented muzzle made it difficult to get the projectile in alone, so Dye rigged a piece of cloth and a rock to seal the vent and went around front to help. The two tried to ram the shot down to no avail. Their efforts ended when another Confederate shell exploded near the gun, wrecking the wheel. As the gun cooled, the shot they were loading became permanently lodged in the barrel. Today the gun is on display at the Statehouse in Providence, Rhode Island.[1] All along this section of the Union line events like this took place, mute testimony to the destructive force of Civil War artillery fire.

It was at the location on which this incident took place that the battery's veterans chose to erect their monument. Basically the main monument is quite plain. At the top is a granite cannon ball beneath which is the trefoil corps symbol. Polished areas on the front and back contain inscriptions that relate the unit's identity and little more. Colonel Brown later purchased a small granite marker to note the position of his battery in the middle of Codori field on the evening of the second. These two memorials were dedicated to the memory of their comrades lost in action.

[1] John H. Rhodes, *The History of Battery B, First Rhode Island Light Artillery, in the War to Preserve the Union, 1861–1865*, (Providence: Snow & Farnham, Printers, 1894), pp. 209–211.

William Jones

Alfred Gardner

BATTERY B's GETTYSBURG GUN

DAN

High Water Mark Memorial

The repulse of Pickett's, Pettigrew's, and Trimble's divisions on the afternoon of July 3 has been termed by historians the symbolic high water mark of the Civil War, that point where the tide of the Confederacy crested and began to recede. As the twenty-fifth anniversary of the battle approached, the Gettysburg Battlefield Memorial Association requested Colonel John B. Bachelder, Superintendent of Tablets and Legends, to prepare a design for a monument to specifically commemorate the High Water Mark. Placed at the copse of oak trees that the men of Pickett's division aimed for, the monument consists of a massive open book propped up by two pyramids of cannonballs. On the pages of the book are the names of the Confederate units that participated in the assault and the Union units that aided in the repulse. The monument was paid for by the fourteen states whose names are listed on the plaque attached beneath the book. Following the monument's dedication, additional plaques were placed on the left and right sides of the base to specifically list the exact regiments that participated in the battle. A plaque on the rear lists the directors of the Memorial Association in 1895. The erection of this monument marked the culmination of the GBMA's efforts at battlefield preservation. The same year the plaque was placed all holdings of the organization were turned over to the federal government to be included as part of the Gettysburg National Military Park.

KLS

LOCATION: COPSE OF TREES, HANCOCK AVENUE
DEDICATED: JUNE 2, 1892
COST: $6,500
DESIGNER: JOHN B. BACHELDER
CONTRACTOR: HENRY BONNARD BRONZE
COMPANY
MATERIAL: BASE—QUINCY GRANITE
PLINTH—FOX ISLAND GRANITE
STANDARD BRONZE
SPECIFICATIONS: SPACE COVERED—48'6" × 18'6"
9'L × 7'4"W

106th Pennsylvania Infantry

Near the High Water Mark Memorial stands one of three monuments honoring the 106th Pennsylvania Infantry. This unit aided in repulsing the attack of Wright's Confederate brigade in the late afternoon of July 2. With the Confederate assault on East Cemetery Hill after dark on July 2, the 106th was shifted to the hill to help in repulsing the Confederate infantry that had gained a foothold among the batteries. On July 3, two companies of the regiment were in position near the angle when Pickett's Charge was launched.

In 1882 a marker was placed at the site of the regiment's services on East Cemetery Hill. Three years later, the Regimental Veteran's Association erected a more substantial monument near the Copse of Trees. This contained an extensive inscription detailing the unit's services during the battle.[1]

When the state monument appropriation became available, the men chose to use it to create the memorial that currently stands near the Copse of Trees. With its erection, the original monument was removed to a site near the Codori house where it was placed on a small plot of land purchased by the Veteran's Association.[2] This monument, of white Westerly granite, features a finely carved sculpture of four knapsacks and blanket rolls which form the base for a stack of three drums. The stacked drums serve to create the trefoil 2nd Corps symbol when viewed from the east or west. This symbol is repeated with the forty carved trefoils that form a band around the shaft, symbolic of the standard forty rounds of ammunition each infantryman carried into battle.

On the front face of the shaft is a highly detailed bronze plaque representing the regiment's charge on the Codori house and barn, the evening of July 2. In this action, the men of the 106th recaptured several cannon of Brown's Rhode Island battery, as well as the Colonel, five captains, fifteen lieutenants, and two hundred fifty men of the 48th Georgia Infantry.[3]

[1] Joseph R. C. Ward, *History of the One Hundred and Sixth Pennsylvania*, (Philadelphia: F. McManus, Jr. & Co., 1906), pp. 386, 391–392.
[2] Ibid., p. 392.
[3] Ibid., pp. 400–401.

LOCATION: HANCOCK AVENUE AT THE ANGLE
DEDICATED: SEPTEMBER 12, 1889
COST: $1,500
SCULPTOR: JOHN WALZ
CONTRACTOR: GRANITE–JOHN M. GESSLER
                BRONZE–BUREAU BROTHERS
MATERIAL: WESTERLY GRANITE
SPECIFICATIONS: 1ST BASE–5'10"SQ × 1'2"H
                    2ND BASE–3'10"SQ × 1'H
                    3RD BASE–3'4"SQ × 1'H
                    DIE–2'10"SQ × 3'3"H
                    CAP–2'6"SQ × 1'6"H
                    TOP–2'2"SQ × 3"H

LS

1st Pennsylvania Cavalry

The men of the 1st Pennsylvania Cavalry were in position during Pickett's Charge just behind the crest of Cemetery Ridge. There they waited in reserve, prepared to attack the Confederate infantry in the event they managed to break through the Union line. Their services were not needed that day as the wave of the Confederate assault broke against the Union infantry regiments, yet the vigilant defiance the men of the 1st exhibited as they anxiously awaited the outcome of the struggle is reflected in their monument today. It consists of a life size bronze statue of a fully equipped cavalryman. Down on one knee, his Sharp's carbine at the ready, he watches for signs of the enemy. A man who served as a private in Company L of the unit that day, Joseph Lindemuth, posed as the model for the statue. On the top of the kepi, the crossed sabre cavalry corps symbol can be seen.

LOCATION: HANCOCK AVENUE AT THE ANGLE
DEDICATED: SEPTEMBER 2, 1890
COST: $1,500
SCULPTOR: H. J. ELLICOTT
CONTRACTOR: BUREAU BROTHERS
MATERIAL: BASE—QUINCY GRANITE
          STANDARD BRONZE
SPECIFICATIONS: 1st BASE—4'4" × 5'3" × 2'
                2ND BASE—3' × 3'1" × 2'

LS

118

72nd Pennsylvania Infantry

The correct placement of monuments on the field was usually achieved through the joint cooperation of the unit's Veteran's Association and the officials of the Gettysburg Battlefield Memorial Association. Occasionally disagreements, hard feelings, and bitterness arose, but only once were feelings raised to such a fevered pitch that it took the legal system to iron out the difficulties. That argument concerned the placement of the monument to the men of the 72nd Pennsylvania Infantry, nicknamed the "Philadelphia Fire Zouaves."

Due to the fame of the High Water Mark / Angle area and its popularity as a stopping point for tours of the field, many units were planning to erect monuments at this site. The G.B.M.A., concerned that the Angle could become overly cluttered, took steps to solve the problem. They ruled that all future monuments had to be placed where the regiment concerned was located in an established line of battle. Preceding Pickett's Charge, the established line of the 72nd Pennsylvania was near present Hancock Avenue, on a line with the 42nd New York and 19th Maine. As Pickett's men surged over the stone wall at the Angle, the 72nd rushed up to aid in throwing the enemy back over the wall. It was at this point the survivors insisted their monument be placed. In the summer of 1888 they proceeded to dig a foundation at that point. This marked the beginning of a fight that would rage through the court system for nearly three years.[1] In the event they managed to lose their case, the men of the 72nd took steps to insure a monument existed near the wall. They purchased a small plot of land from the Codori farm, still privately owned at that time. If the case was decided against them, they were fully determined to erect their monument west of the stone wall. The issue was eventually carried to the Pennsylvania Supreme Court which upheld the lower court decisions allowing the Regiment's monument to be placed at the stone wall.[2]

In the summer of 1891 the monument was finally erected. It consists of a statue of an infantryman clothed in the uniform of a Philadelphia Fire Zouave. Designed by J. Reed, a former private in the 72nd, it portrays a youthful soldier: twelve hundred of the regiment's fourteen hundred men were under the age of twenty-one.[3] The pose of the soldier clubbing with his musket was designed to depict the closeness of the fighting at the wall as they struggled with the men of Pickett's division.

[1] *Pennsylvania at Gettysburg,* 1:416–417.

[2] Ibid. There was considerable bitterness over this decision on the part of other regiments who also desired their monuments be placed at the wall. See *New York at Gettysburg,* 1:328.

[3] *Pennsylvania at Gettysburg,* 1:416.

LOCATION: WEBB AVENUE AT THE ANGLE
DEDICATED: JULY 4, 1891
SCULPTOR: STEPHENS
DESIGNER: J. REED
CONTRACTOR: WILLIAM BLAKE AND FOUNDERS

LS

119

71st Pennsylvania Infantry

On the capstone of the monument honoring the men of the 71st Pennsylvania Infantry is the curious designation "California Regiment." In the early weeks of the Civil War, a group of Californians in Washington wished to have their state represented in the armies being formed in the east. Senator Edward D. Baker of Oregon was persuaded to undertake the task of organizing a new regiment to be credited to the state of California. Recruiting offices were set up in New York City and Philadelphia and, in a short time, a large regiment was raised and given the designation 1st California Infantry. Nine of the original companies came from Philadelphia and one from New York. Eventually four more California regiments were recruited, primarily in Pennsylvania. Following Colonel Baker's death at the battle of Ball's Bluff in the fall of 1861, the regiments were all claimed by the state of Pennsylvania as part of their quota and the 1st California was redesignated the 71st Pennsylvania Infantry.[1] The nickname "California Regiment" remained and was proudly inscribed on their monument at Gettysburg. The 71st and the other California regiments, now redesignated 69th Pennsylvania (2nd Cal.), 72nd Pennsylvania (3rd Cal.), and 106th Pennsylvania (5th Cal.), were grouped in a single brigade known as the Philadelphia Brigade; the only brigade in either army to bear the name of a city.

The monument to the 71st Pennsylvania is somewhat plain, bearing on the capstone the two nicknames of the unit and the words 'Heroism' and 'Patriotism'. A rather detailed description of the unit's actions in the battle and its association with Colonel Baker fill the four faces of the die.

[1] Frank H. Taylor, *Philadelphia in the Civil War 1861–1865*, (Philadelphia: Printed by the city, 1913), pp. 85–86, 89–90.

REF

LOCATION: WEBB AVENUE, THE ANGLE
DEDICATED: JUNE 30, 1887
COST: $1,754
DESIGNER/CONTRACTOR: SMITH GRANITE CO
MATERIAL: BLUE WESTERLY GRANITE
SPECIFICATIONS: 6'6"SQ × 10'5"H

1st Andrews Sharpshooters (Massachusetts)

The monument to the 1st company of Andrews Sharpshooters consists of a block of Italian marble carved to resemble a rubble wall. On the die is a figure of a sharpshooter aiming his rifle at the enemy. The weapon he is using is a heavy sharpshooter's rifle especially designed for accuracy and range. Men using such weapons were the scourge of the infantrymen and artillerymen who hated the deceitful, cowardly, and "unchristianly" style of fighting practiced by sharpshooter units. Candidates for these regiments were required to place ten shots in a ten inch circle at two hundred yards, using any firing position and any type of rifle they desired.[1] Such individuals well-positioned, could wreak havoc on a battlefield picking off high ranking officers,

members of gun crews, and carelessly exposed infantrymen. One interesting feature of the weapon depicted on the Andrews Sharpshooters monument is the crude telescopic sight that runs the length of the octagonal barrel. It would not have allowed for the degree of magnification of today's scope but it still allowed for somewhat more accurate sighting. The slogan inscribed on the monument, "In God We Put Our Trust, But Kept Our Powder Dry," appropriately sums up the attitude of the men who made up this specialized and somewhat despised branch of service.

[1] Faust, *Encyclopedia of the Civil War*, pp. 671–672.

LOCATION: HANCOCK AVENUE
DEDICATED: 1886
COST: $500
MATERIAL: ITALIAN MARBLE

LS

121

Battery K, 1st New York Artillery

At one o'clock on the afternoon of July 3, a massive artillery bombardment commenced as one hundred thirty-eight Confederate cannon shelled the Union center. Several batteries were smashed during the course of the two hour bombardment. One of the Union batteries sent in to replace those disabled was Captain Robert H. Fitzhugh's Battery K, 1st New York Artillery. During the course of the action that day, they fired nearly ninety shells at the enemy.[1]

The main feature on the monument to Battery K is a large bronze plaque depicting an artillery piece being loaded. The gun represented is an Ordnance rifle, the type of piece the battery was equipped with. Four members of the gun crew are represented in the plaque. Number 1 is sponging out the barrel from the last discharge, while number 5 is carrying the next round up. Number 3 thumbs the vent and the gunner prepares to give the order to fire.

[1] *New York at Gettysburg*, 3:1251.

KLS

LOCATION: HANCOCK AVENUE
DEDICATED: JULY 2, 1888
COST: $1,500
SCULPTOR: STEPHEN J. O'KELLY
DESIGNER/CONTRACTOR: FREDERICK & FIELD
MATERIAL: QUINCY GRANITE
         STANDARD BRONZE
SPECIFICATIONS: BASE–7'L × 4'6"W × 9'H
         BRONZE PLAQUE–4'L × 3'9"W
         TABLET–2'6"SQ

39th New York Infantry (Garibaldi Guards)

At the beginning of the Civil War, the Union Defense Committee of New York authorized the raising of a regiment composed of European refugees and immigrants to fight for their adopted country. The plan involved recruiting three companies of Hungarians, three companies of Germans, and one company each of Italians, Swiss, French, and Spanish/Portuguese. Although they never quite attained the pure companies originally planned, the 39th had quite a mixture of nationalities.[1] The nickname of the regiment, Garibaldi Guards, came from the Italian revolutionary Guiseppe Garibaldi who had contributed greatly to the unification of the Italian states. By 1863 the Gari-

baldis were reduced to four companies of about three hundred men.[2]

The monument to the Garibaldi Guards is a plain one consisting of a large granite shaft topped by a trefoil corps symbol. A bronze plaque on the back gives a very brief history of the unit's activities in the battle. South of this position, near United States Avenue, a second marker identifies the spot where the unit recaptured a Union battery on the evening of July 2.

[1] *New York at Gettysburg*, I:282.
[2] Ibid., p. 279.

LOCATION: NORTH HANCOCK AVENUE
DEDICATED: JULY 1, 1888
COST: $1,500
DESIGNER/CONTRACTOR: FREDERICK & FIELD
MATERIAL: 1ST BASE–GETTYSBURG GRANITE
                SHAFT–QUINCY GRANITE
SPECIFICATIONS: 7'SQ × 20'H
                     TABLET–2'41/2 × 2'

KLS

1st Delaware Infantry

As the North Carolinians of Johnston Pettigrew's division hurled themselves at the stone wall constituting the Union defense line, one unit that met the advance was the 1st Delaware Infantry. The 1st Delaware was one of two regiments from that state to participate in the battle. They had the unique experience of leading a countercharge over the wall which resulted in the capture of several Confederate battle-flags and more prisoners than the 1st Delaware had men in their command. Gettysburg would cost the unit seventy-seven casualties and by battle's end, a lieutenant, the highest ranking, unwounded officer, was placed in command.

In the spring of 1885, a committee of regimental survivors was appointed to go to Gettysburg and select a site for the unit's monument. The location chosen was where the men countercharged over the wall in pursuit of the Confederates. The monument is a simple one of Brandywine blue granite and includes a very sketchy inscription. The only ornamentations present are the highly polished trefoil 2nd Corps symbols on each face of the capstone and a polished diamond shape on the front. This was designed to represent one of Delaware's nicknames, the "Diamond State."

LOCATION: HANCOCK AVENUE
DEDICATED: JUNE 10, 1886
COST: $425
DESIGNER/CONTRACTOR: THOMAS DAVIDSON
MATERIAL: BRANDYWINE BLUE GRANITE
SPECIFICATIONS: 4'6"SQ × 7'6"H

LS

George Gordon Meade Equestrian Statue

At a point just behind the Angle, the statue of the Army of the Potomac's commander, Major-General George Gordon Meade, gazes out over the field where his Union army won one of the greatest battles of the Civil War. It honors a man who not only won this crucial battle, but was able to successfully lead the army through the next two years of the war. Unfortunately he is often overshadowed today by the General-in-chief of all Union armies, Ulysses S. Grant, who chose to travel with Meade's army.

Meade, who assumed command of the army just two days prior to the battle, is depicted bareheaded, as he looked on that July afternoon, riding up the ridge towards the angle just as the Confederate charge is being turned back. It was in this general vicinity that Meade arrived shortly after the repulse.

Here he accepted the jubilant shouts of his victorious army.[1]

The statue was the work of sculptor Henry K. Bush-Brown, the same individual who also worked on the Reynolds Equestrian. Brown spent nearly two years researching and creating this piece.[2] The Meade statue is approximately eight-tenths of a mile across from that of his adversary, Robert E. Lee, atop the Virginia Memorial. These two opponents eternally face each other across the fields where their armies clashed.

[1] *Pennsylvania at Gettysburg*, 2:955; Vanderslice, *Gettysburg: Then and Now*, p. 448.

[2] Craven, *Sculptures at Gettysburg*, p. 44. This contains a very good account of how an equestrian statue like that of Meade is created.

LOCATION: HANCOCK AVENUE
DEDICATED: JUNE 5, 1896
COST: $37,500
SCULPTOR: HENRY KIRKE BUSH-BROWN
CONTRACTOR: BUREAU BROTHERS
MATERIAL: STANDARD BRONZE

FWH

12th New Jersey Infantry

The 12th New Jersey Infantry was involved in the fighting along this line on July 2 and July 3. Twice during this time, detachments of the regiment were sent out into the Bliss farm, beyond the Emmitsburg Road, to clear the buildings of Confederate Sharpshooters. On July 2, the 12th New Jersey had captured seven officers and eighty-five men of the Confederate skirmish line at the farm. In a second assault on the morning of July 3, the Bliss buildings were captured a second time and burned. During the cannonade preceding Pickett's Charge, the regiment lay in position behind the stone wall. Armed with old .69 caliber smoothbore muskets, the men knew the Confederates would have to come within one hundred yards of the wall before their muskets would be effective. Even then they were highly inaccurate. To compensate for this, they had been issued "Buck and Ball" cartridges consisting of one round ball that fit the bore and three small buckshot. To further increase their odds, the men of the 12th New Jersey

FWH

used the time prior to the charge to tear the cartridges apart, throw the ball away, and load the muskets with up to twenty-five buckshot. These they used with great effectiveness when the charge finally came

In the early 1880's the Veteran's Association of the regiment raised the necessary funds to place a monument on the field, becoming the first New Jersey unit to do so.[1] The state appropriation permitted the veterans to place a small memorial at the site of the Bliss buildings and to upgrade the main monument. In accomplishing this, they added a bronze plaque depicting the regiment's charge on the Confederate skirmishers and sharpshooters at the Bliss house and barn. On top of the monument sits a highly polished example of a "Buck and Ball" charge. An inscription on the face of the monument also refers to this ammunition, evidence of the significance this item had to the men of the 12th New Jersey.

[1] Toombs, *New Jersey Troops in the Gettysburg Campaign*, pp. 333, 337.

KLS

LOCATION: NORTH HANCOCK AVENUE
DEDICATED: MAY 26, 1886
COST: $1,000
SCULPTOR: BEATTIE AND BROOKS
DESIGNER/CONTRACTOR: MICHAEL REILLY
MATERIAL: RICHMOND GRANITE
SPECIFICATIONS: BASE—4'8"SQ × 2'
                         2ND BASE—3'8"SQ × 18"
                         DIE—2'8"SQ × 4'10"
                         CAPSTONE/TREFOIL—3'2" SQ × 2'
                         OVERALL HEIGHT—12'6"

111th New York Infantry

At the wall near the Brien barn, the monument of the 111th New York Infantry stands topped by the statue of an infantry skirmisher. The members of the regiment's monument committee felt that this was the most appropriate design as they entered the battle as skirmishers. These were individuals deployed in scattered bodies in advance of the main battle line in order to provide an early warning system. Elements of the 111th New York served as skirmishers throughout the battle.[1]

The monument of the unit is erected on the spot where the regimental colors stood during the battle. On this site, four color bearers and two officers were killed during Pickett's Charge. The skirmisher atop the base is portrayed as advancing forward into the fields. His cap is thrown back to clear his vision.[2] Knowing that on the skirmish line fighting could erupt at any minute, he is cocking the trigger prepared to fire at any sign of enemy movement.

[1] *New York at Gettysburg*, 2:803.
[2] Ibid.

LOCATION: NORTH HANCOCK AVENUE
           AT THE BRIEN BARN
DEDICATED: JUNE 26, 1891
COST: $2,400
SCULPTOR: CASPAR BUBERL
CONTRACTOR: BASE–FREDERICK & FIELD
           STATUE–HENRY BONNARD
           BRONZE CO.
MATERIAL: QUINCY GRANITE
           STANDARD BRONZE
SPECIFICATIONS: BASE–8'2" × 5'10"
           HEIGHT–14'3"
           STATUE–3' × 2'2" ×6'9"
           TABLET–2'9" × 1'10"

KLS

Grand Army of the Republic Memorial (Albert Woolson)

For years following the Civil War, one of the most powerful groups in the United States was the Union veteran's organization known as the Grand Army of the Republic. Roughly equivalent of today's American Legion or Veterans of Foreign Wars, GAR Posts were found in just about every northern town. They were dedicated to helping the war vets, commemorating the struggle, and providing the camaraderie and fellowship army-life had nurtured. Therefore, it was appropriate that one of the last northern monuments on the field at Gettysburg would be a memorial to this organization.

The monument stands in Zeigler's Grove near the park's Cyclorama building and consists of an old veteran on a bench looking out over the fields where Pickett's Charge had swept. The man depicted is Albert Woolson of Duluth, Minnesota. He played no role in the battle of Gettysburg, yet his statue is quite appropriate on this field. As a teenager, he had enlisted in the 1st Minnesota Heavy Artillery during the latter stages of the war. Joining the Grand Army of the Republic, as many of his fellow comrades did, he participated in many reunions such as the large anniversary gatherings held at Gettysburg in 1913 and 1938. In 1956, Woolson died at the age of 109 having outlived all other men who had served in the Union armed forces during the Civil War. With his passing, the GAR also passed out of existence. Later that year, the successor organization to the GAR, the Sons of Union Veterans of the Civil War, erected the monument to the memory of Woolson and the more than 2.2 million men who served with him in the defense of the American Union between 1861 and 1865.

LS

LOCATION: HANCOCK AVENUE (ZEIGLER'S GROVE)
DEDICATED: SEPTEMBER 12, 1956
SCULPTOR: AVARD FAIRBANKS
DESIGNER/CONTRACTOR: ROMAN BRONZE WORKS
MATERIAL: COLD SPRINGS GRANITE
          STANDARD BRONZE

SECTION SIX: THE NATIONAL CEMETERY

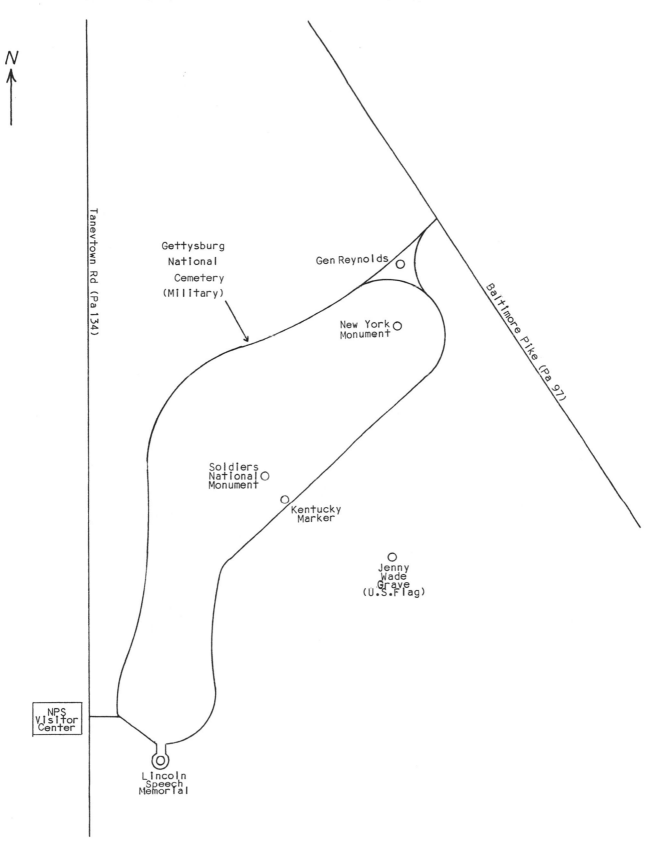

N

Tanevtown Rd (Pa 134)

Gettysburg National Cemetery (Military)

Gen Reynolds

Baltimore Pike (Pa 97)

New York Monument

Soldiers National Monument

Kentucky Marker

Jenny Wade Grave (U.S.Flag)

NPS Visitor Center

Lincoln Speech Memorial

Lincoln Speech Memorial

The bill of Representative Daniel Sickles, passed into law February 11, 1895, created the Gettysburg National Military Park. It also contained a provision for the creation of a memorial tablet commemorating the Gettysburg Address. Nearly $5,000 was appropriated to accomplish this. Designed by Louis Henrick, the monument consists of a curved wall containing two bronze plaques. On the left is the letter of Judge David Wills to Abraham Lincoln, inviting the president to come to Gettysburg. The plaque on the right contains a copy of the Gettysburg Address. Flanking each plaque are bundles of fasces with protruding ax heads, the ancient symbol of strength and unity.[1]

The stars carved above the plaques are representative of the states that remained loyal to the union.

The central feature of the monument is a bust of Abraham Lincoln sculpted by Henry Bush-Brown. It was decided not to pursue a full portrait statue as it would detract from the theme of the monument. Disagreements over where to locate the memorial delayed its construction for nearly a decade. It was finally completed in 1912. Today, it stands as one of the few memorials in the world built to honor a speech.

[1] Craven, *Sculptures at Gettysburg*, p. 32.

LS

LOCATION: NATIONAL CEMETERY
ERECTED: JANUARY 24, 1912
DEDICATED: NEVER
COST: $5,000
SCULPTOR: HENRY KIRKE BUSH-BROWN
DESIGNER: LOUIS R. HENRICK
CONTRACTOR: VAN AMRINGE GRANITE CO.

Soldiers National Monument

The first memorial of any type to be placed at Gettysburg was the Soldiers National Monument in the National Cemetery. Part of the original plan for the cemetery, laid out by landscape architect William Saunders, called for the creation of a large memorial in the center of the semi-circle of Union graves. Designed by the Batterson-Canfield Company, the cornerstone was laid on July 4, 1865, just three months after the close of the war.[1] The monument consists of a large pedestal of white Westerly granite which supports a shaft and marble statue entitled "Genius of Liberty." Around the shaft, a band of eighteen bronze stars honors the loyal states represented in the army at Gettysburg. The coat of arms beneath them is the symbol of the Union that was preserved here. Liberty rests on a three-quarter globe as she clutches a sword in her left hand. Her right hand holds the victor's laurel wreath, classical symbol of victory.

On each of the four buttresses are allegorical statues in white marble, carved in Italy under the direction of sculptor Randolph Rogers. On the left side of the front face is "War," portrayed as an American soldier resting after the conflict. The panels on either side of his chair contain the tools of warfare, while his foot rests on an artillery tube. He is relating the story of what happened here to the second, statue, "History," as she records the achievements and the names of the dead in her book. Beneath her foot rests a stack of books, the record of past events. On the right side of her chair, the pyramid and palm tree symbolize man's heritage, while the crumbling columns on the left represent the result of man's vanity and ambition.

The back face of the monument contains the statue of "Plenty" as she symbolizes the peace and abundance brought about as a result of the soldier's triumph here. The sheath of wheat over her arm and the cornucopias filled with the fruits of the earth are all symbolic of the abundance of this nation. The final statue symbolizes peace. It represents a mechanic and features the tools of the trade, machine

LOCATION: NATIONAL CEMETERY
DEDICATED: JULY 1, 1869
COST: $50,000
SCULPTOR: RANDOLPH ROGERS
DESIGNER: JAMES GOODWIN BATTERSON
CONTRACTOR: NEW ENGLAND GRANITE WORKS
MATERIAL: WHITE WESTERLY GRANITE
        ITALIAN CARRERA MARBLE
SPECIFICATIONS: BASE–25'SQ
             HEIGHT–60'

LS

LS

131

cogs and heavy hammers. Perhaps the most unusual of the five statues, "Peace" is represented here as a man where classical statues universally portrayed peace as a woman.

The panel on the back face contains the last part of Lincoln's Gettysburg Address, delivered nearby. On July 1, 1869, the sixth anniversary of the start of the battle, the Soldiers National Monument was dedicated with great ceremony.

[1] Craven, *Sculptures at Gettysburg*, p. 12. The inscription "Batterson Fecit" on the lower right corner of the front base is translated "Batterson Made It." Craven believes it may actually have been designed by an employee of Batterson, George Kelly.

Kentucky State Monument

Kentucky was a border state during the Civil War and divisions ran deep. Soldiers from the state enlisted in both northern and southern armies. Few, however, fought in the eastern theater of war and no Kentucky regiments fought at Gettysburg. The state was also the birthplace of both Confederate president Jefferson Davis and President Abraham Lincoln. It was this latter relationship that led to the creation of the Kentucky monument. In the early 1970's a movement was begun to raise money to place a memorial near the site where Lincoln delivered the Gettysburg Address. The monument contains the Bliss copy of the address on a bronze plaque. It was the last of the five copies of the address actually written by Lincoln and the only one that he signed. Written for inclusion in a book published for charitable purposes, the copy today hangs in the Lincoln Room of the White House. The Kentucky Monument was dedicated on the 112th anniversary of the delivery of the address, November 19, 1975.

LS

LOCATION: NATIONAL CEMETERY
DEDICATED: NOVEMBER 19, 1975
SPECIFICATIONS: 51"L × 27 1/2"W × 12"–21"H

Jennie Wade's Grave

Mary Virginia Wade was the only local civilian to lose her life in the battle of Gettysburg. She and her mother came to the small house on the slope of Cemetery Hill to take care of her sister, Georgia Wade McClellan who had just given birth. At about 8 A.M. on the morning of July 3, Jenny Wade was preparing dough to make biscuits when a stray sharpshooter's bullet came through two doors and struck her in the back, killing the twenty year old girl instantly. She was buried the following day outside Georgia's house. In early 1864, the body was moved to a cemetery in town and, following the war, she was moved a third time to her present resting place in Evergreen Cemetery.[1]

Just after the war the McClellans moved to Iowa where Georgia became involved in the Women's Relief Corps. In the WRC convention of 1900, a vote was taken to erect a statue over the grave of Georgia's sister. Contributions were solicited and Anna Miller was chosen to execute the statue that now exists. It was dedicated on September 16, 1901 in the presence of many members of the Iowa Relief Corps including Georgia McClellan. Nine years later, the Gettysburg Association of Iowa Women purchased and placed a steel flagstaff on the grave. On this pole an American flag is permitted by law to fly day and night. Each year, the Women's Relief Corps sends two new flags to fly over the grave.[2]

[1] J. W. Johnston, *The True Story of "Jennie" Wade—A Gettysburg Maid*, (Rochester: the author, 1918), p. 28.
[2] Ibid., p. 29.

LOCATION: EVERGREEN CEMETERY
DEDICATED: SEPTEMBER 16, 1901
COST: $1,200
SCULPTOR: ANNA MILLER

LS

133

New York State Monument

By 1892, the state of New York had aided in constructing a monument on the battlefield at Gettysburg for each of the state's regiments and batteries that fought here. These monuments were intended to honor all New Yorkers, both living and dead, that participated in the battle. The New York Monuments Commission felt that a massive state memorial, specifically to honor New York's battle dead, was needed to complete the job. In 1893, the present monument was erected and dedicated forever overlooking the New York plot in the National Cemetery.

It consists of a massive base which supports a large column. Bronze plaques on the base contain the names of every New York officer killed at Gettysburg. Above the plaque are individual corps badges which appear on monuments throughout the field. These represent, left to right, the 1st, 2nd, 3rd, 5th, 6th, 11th, and 12th army corps, the cavalry, engineers, signal corps, and artillery. New York's soldiers were well represented in each of these organizations.

The base of the thirty-three foot high column contains a four section alto relievo representing generals from New York during key moments in the battle. The four scenes are entitled: "The Wounding of General Sickles," an event that occurred during the July 2 evening battle on the south end of the field; "The Wounding of General Hancock," which took place during Pickett's Charge, July 3; "General Slocum's Council of War," a key event prior to the seven hour battle for Culp's Hill on the morning of July 3; and "The Death of General Reynolds," from the first day's battle.[1] Dividing each panel is a collection of war material from each branch of service. A pile of artillery relics is carved to the left of "Sickles," while the equipment of a cavalryman fills the space between "Hancock" and "Slocum." To the left of "Slocum," the boundary consists of infantry implements and the tools of the engineers are stacked between "Reynolds" and "Sickles."

The column itself is part Ionic and part Corinthian in design. At the front base is a bronze seal of the state of New York above which is a large eagle with outstretched wings perched in front of a series of battleflags, trophies of war won by New Yorkers on many battlefields. The statue resting atop the shaft is based on the female figure on the left side of the New York state seal.[2] Representing the state of New York, the figure is portrayed as crying over the

LS

LOCATION: NATIONAL CEMETERY
DEDICATED: JULY 2, 1893
COST: $59,095
SCULPTOR: CASPAR BUBERL
DESIGNER: MARSHALL AND WALTER
CONTRACTOR: GRANITE - HALLOWELL GRANITE
        CO.
        BRONZE - HENRY BONNARD
        BRONZE CO. (STATUE, ALTO
        RELIEVO, TABLETS)
        BRONZE - MAURICE POWERS
        (TROPHY, SEAL, CORPS BADGES)
MATERIAL: HALLOWELL GRANITE
        STANDARD BRONZE
SPECIFICATIONS: BASE—27'8"SQ
        PLINTH—3'1"H
        SHAFT—5'6" DIA TAPERING
        33' HIGH
        STATUE—13'H 6200 POUNDS
        ALTO RELIEVO—19'8 1/2" DIA
        5'6"H

state's battle dead. In her right hand she holds a wreath of flowers to place on the graves.[3] The staff in her left hand is topped by a Liberty Cap, a type of stocking cap that served as a long time symbol of freedom. Here at Gettysburg, many New Yorkers paid the supreme price to preserve the Union that had made freedom and individual rights a cornerstone of its existence.

[1] The following generals are portrayed on each segment: "Sickles"–Generals Carr, Ward, Graham, Ayres, Weed, Zook, and Tremain; "Hancock"–Generals Butterfield, Warren, Kilpatrick, Webb; "Slocum"–Generals Pleasonton, Wadsworth, Greene, Hunt, Bartlett, Russell, Shaler, and Barnum; "Reynolds"–Generals Doubleday, Von Steinwehr, Robinson, Barlow, Devin.
[2] Craven, *Sculptures at Gettysburg*, p. 20.
[3] *New York at Gettysburg*, 1:236.

John F. Reynolds Portrait Statue

The statue of General John F. Reynolds was the first portrait statue to be erected at Gettysburg. Following his death, members of the general's personal staff developed an idea to mark the spot where he fell with a simple memorial. At a meeting of the officers of Reynolds's 1st Corps in January 1864, a committee was appointed and funds solicited from the men Reynolds had led.[1] Contributions were limited to no more than five dollars from each officer and fifty cents per enlisted man. More than $5,700 was collected in this manner.[2] As the war was nearing its end, the exact monument site was chosen in the National Cemetery.

As the nation settled back into peacetime pursuits, the Reynold's Memorial Committee was still active. In 1867, the decision was reached to create a bronze portrait statue to honor the general. The state of Pennsylvania contributed bronze cannon to be melted down while the National Cemetery managers donated the site and funds to erect the base. Sketches were made, plaster models inspected, sculptors chosen, and contracts signed. The statue was cast in Philadelphia in 1872 and exhibited for a time in the city. The railroad transported it to Gettysburg free of charge where it was erected in the summer of 1872, nine years after Reynold's death.[3]

Modeled from a photograph of the general, it depicts Reynolds as he may have appeared that day: field glasses in hand, watching the movements of the enemy and contemplating what moves to take. At the selected location, the statue was placed so it looks out over the field on which he fell.

[1] John B. Bachelder, *Gettysburg: What to see and how to see it*, (New York: Lee, Shepard, and Dillingham, 1873), pp. 118–119.
[2] Ibid.
[3] Ibid., Craven, *Sculptures at Gettysburg*, p. 56.

LOCATION: NATIONAL CEMETERY
DEDICATED: AUGUST 31, 1872
COST: $15,037
SCULPTOR: J. Q. A. WARD
DESIGNER: RICHARD MORRIS HUNT
CONTRACTOR: ROBERT WOOD AND COMPANY
MATERIAL: DARK QUINCY GRANITE
STANDARD BRONZE
SPECIFICATIONS: BASE–10'H 23 TONS
STATUE–8'H

KLS

SELECTED
BIBLIOGRAPHY

Commission for Illinois Monuments at Gettysburg. *Illinois at Gettysburg: The Final Report of the Battlefield Commissioners.* Springfield: H. W. Rokker, State Printer and Binder, 1892.

Coddington, Edwin B. *The Gettysburg Campaign: A Study in Command.* Dayton: Press of the Morningside Bookshop, 1979.

Craven, Wayne. *The Sculptures at Gettysburg.* Eastern Acorn Press, 1982.

Davis, William C. *Gettysburg: The Story Behind the Scenery.* Las Vegas: K.C. Publications, Inc., 1983.

Faust, Patricia L., ed., *Historical Times Illustrated Encyclopedia of the Civil War.* New York: Harper and Row, 1986.

Gettysburg National Military Park Commission. *Annual Reports of the Gettysburg National Military Park Commission to the Secretary of War, 1893–1904.* Washington: Government Printing Office, 1905.

Maine Gettysburg Monuments Commission, *Maine at Gettysburg: Report of the Maine Commissioners Prepared by the Executive Committee.* Portland: The Lakeside Press, 1898.

Martin, David G. *Confederate Monuments at Gettysburg.* Hightstown, N.J.: Longstreet House, 1986.

Michigan Monument Commission. *Michigan at Gettysburg, July 1st, 2nd, and 3rd, 1863, June 12th, 1889.* Detroit: Winn and Hammond, Printers and Binders, 1889.

New Jersey Battlefield Monuments Commission. *Final Report of the Gettysburg Battlefield Commission of New Jersey, dated October 1, 1891.* Trenton, N.J.: The John L. Murphy Publishing Co., 1891.

New Jersey Battlefield Monuments Commission. *Report of the Commissioners to care for Gettysburg Battle Monuments, 1892.* Trenton, N.J.: Naar, Day, and Naas, Printers, 1893.

New York Monuments Commission for the Battlefields of Gettysburg and Chattanooga. *New York at Gettysburg: The Final Report on the Battlefield at Gettysburg.* 3 volumes. Albany: J.B. Lyon Company, Printers, 1902.

Ohio Gettysburg Memorial Commission. *Report of the Gettysburg Memorial Commission.* Columbus: Press of the Nitschke Brothers, 1889.

Pennsylvania State Monuments Commission. *Pennsylvania at Gettysburg: Ceremonies at the Dedication of the Monuments.* 3 volumes. Harrisburg: William Stanley Ray, State Printer, 1914.

Vanderslice, John M. *Gettysburg Then and Now.* New York: G. W. Dillingham, 1899. Reprinted Dayton, Ohio: Morningside Bookshop Press, 1983.

Vermont Gettysburg Monuments Commission. *Report of the Vermont Commissioners 1890 Including the Speeches and Poem at the Dedication October 9, 1889.* Burlington: The Free Press Association, 1890.

War of the Rebellion: The Official Records of the Union and Confederate Armies. Series I, Volume XXVII, Part 1. Washington: Government Printing Office, 1889.

INDEX